IoT Product Development Using ESP32 Microcontrollers

A Staggered Approach with Six Prototyping and Product Development Examples

Sai Yamanoor
Srihari Yamanoor

Apress®

IoT Product Development Using ESP32 Microcontrollers: A Staggered Approach with Six Prototyping and Product Development Examples

Sai Yamanoor
Santa Clara, CA, USA

Srihari Yamanoor
Vallejo, CA, USA

ISBN-13 (pbk): 979-8-8688-1569-0
https://doi.org/10.1007/979-8-8688-1570-6

ISBN-13 (electronic): 979-8-8688-1570-6

Managing Director, Apress Media LLC: Welmoed Spahr
Acquisitions Editor: Spandana Chatterjee
Coordinating Editor: Gryffin Winkler

Cover designed by eStudioCalamar

Cover image by Vishnu Mohanan unsplash (unsplash.com)

Distributed to the book trade worldwide by Springer Science+Business Media New York, 1 New York Plaza, New York, NY 10004. Phone 1-800-SPRINGER, fax (201) 348-4505, e-mail orders-ny@springer-sbm.com, or visit www.springeronline.com. Apress Media, LLC is a Delaware LLC and the sole member (owner) is Springer Science + Business Media Finance Inc (SSBM Finance Inc). SSBM Finance Inc is a **Delaware** corporation.

For information on translations, please e-mail booktranslations@springernature.com; for reprint, paperback, or audio rights, please e-mail bookpermissions@springernature.com.

Apress titles may be purchased in bulk for academic, corporate, or promotional use. eBook versions and licenses are also available for most titles. For more information, reference our Print and eBook Bulk Sales web page at http://www.apress.com/bulk-sales.

Any source code or other supplementary material referenced by the author in this book is available to readers on GitHub (https://github.com/Apress). For more detailed information, please visit https://www.apress.com/gp/services/source-code.

If disposing of this product, please recycle the paper

This book is dedicated to all Makers who like to start
multiple projects on a whim...

Table of Contents

About the Authors.. xi

About the Technical Reviewer xiii

Acknowledgments...xv

Introduction xvii

Chapter 1: Introduction to the ESP32 Platform 1

Introduction to the ESP32 Platform.. 2

    ESP32 Microcontroller Variants 2

Advantages of the ESP32 Platform 3

ESP32 Development Board Selection... 7

    ESP32 Module Variant Selection... 7

    ESP32 Development Board Selection 8

Tour of the Adafruit Metro ESP32-S3 Development Board............................ 12

Programming Language Options and Selection... 15

    Programming Language Selection 16

    Integrated Development Environment Installation 17

    Arduino IDE.. 22

Documents to Download 25

First Programming Example... 25

    LED Blinky Using MicroPython... 25

    LED Blinky Using the Arduino IDE 31

Wi-Fi Examples 35

    Wi-Fi Scanner.. 35

    Connecting to Wi-Fi 37

Testing ESP32's Bluetooth Capabilities.. 39

Conclusion 44

Chapter 2: Building a Weather Station 45

Description 45

    Components Used in This Project 47

Use Case 47

    Weather Sensor Selection 47

Sensor Integration 48

    Introduction to the UART Interface 48

    Setting Up the UART Interface 49

Publishing Data to the Cloud 53

    Creating secrets.py 56

    Publishing Data Using Webhooks 58

Dashboard Setup 64

    Dashboard Considerations 69

Installation Considerations 69

Conclusion 69

Chapter 3: Visual Aid for Air Quality 71

Project Description 71

    Product Case 72

    Components Used in This Project 73

Retrieving Data Using an API 74

    Obtaining an API Key 75

    Performing a Test Query 75

    MicroPython Code for Retrieving AQI Data 79

    Data Use Guidelines 88

Interfacing Air Quality Sensors to the ESP32 89

    Sensor Selection 89

    I^2C Communication Interface 90

    Qwiic Connect System 91

    Drivers for SCD41 and SEN55 95

    MicroPython I^2C Driver for SCD41 and SEN55 96

Installing Prerequisite Libraries..96

Modifying I²C Drivers for Sensirion Sensors...98

SEN55 MicroPython Driver 100

SCD41 MicroPython Driver 105

Building the Visual Aid 108

Display Setup..108

Visual Aid Code...110

LVGL...114

Challenge...115

Taking Your Visual Aid to Market..115

Revenue Model..115

Product Pricing 115

Enclosure 115

Sourcing Components 116

Manufacturing...116

Device Provisioning 116

Time to Market 116

Servicing 117

Conclusion 117

Chapter 4: Building Bluetooth Products Using ESP32 119

Bluetooth Low Energy 119

BLE on ESP32 119

Components Required..120

Sensor Integration...120

Sensor Drivers...122

Driver Test...122

Bluetooth Sensor Node...124

Bluetooth/Wi-Fi Gateway Using ESP32 136

Power Profiling for Low-Power Applications..140

Conclusion 142

Chapter 5: Low-Power and Long-Range Radios with ESP32 143

LoRa Radios 143

Required Components 143

Interfacing LoRa Radios to ESP32-S3 144

    Library Installation 144

    Antenna Assembly 145

    Wiring Up the RFM95W Breakout 146

    Testing the Breakout Board 148

    Sensor Data Aggregation and Publishing to the Cloud 152

Publishing Data to LoRaWAN Networks 162

    Interfacing Cellular Modules to the ESP32 163

Compliance Engineering 164

Conclusion 165

Chapter 6: Building TinyML Products 167

What Is TinyML? 167

    Need for TinyML 167

TinyML Toolsets 171

Image Classification Example Using Edge Impulse 172

    Hardware Requirements 172

TinyML Audio Application Example 194

    Schematic 195

    Code Sample Modification 196

    Description of the Example 196

    Prerequisite Installation 196

TinyML Product Development Challenges 200

Conclusion 201

Chapter 7: Let's Build a Product! 203

Components Required 204

Capturing Product Requirements 204

Breadboarding a Prototype 205

Sensor Selection... 205

MAX30102 205

TMP117 205

Schematic Capture.. 205

ESP32-Module Selection 206

Filtering and Decoupling capacitors.. 207

Reset Circuit 207

Bootstrapping Pins 208

I²C Circuit... 209

Debugging Circuitry... 209

USB Interface... 209

Debug LED 210

Interrupt Pins... 210

Real-Time Clock 211

TMP117 Sensor 211

MAX30102 Sensor 212

Qwiic Sensor Interface 213

Power Circuitry... 214

Electrical Rule Check.. 217

PCB Layout.. 218

Enclosure Selection.. 218

Board Shape Import.. 219

Component Placement and Layout.. 219

Quote Generation... 226

Assembly Confirmation 227

Board Bring-Up 227

Testing Sensors 231

Power Profiling.. 238

Product Development Considerations 238

Component Placement 239

Redundant Components 239

Enclosure Cutouts...239

Display Interface..239

Project Complications..240

Compliance Engineering...240

Battery Selection 240

Enclosure Assembly...240

Conclusion 241

Index...**243**

About the Authors

Sai Yamanoor is an Embedded Engineer based in Santa Clara, California. He has over ten years of experience as an embedded systems expert, working on hardware, firmware, and software design and implementations. He is a co-author of three books on using Raspberry Pi to execute DIY projects and has also presented DIY IoT projects at international conferences and Maker Faires. Sai is also working on projects to improve quality of life for people with chronic health conditions. Sai also enjoys collaborating and creating citizen science projects to benefit general public of various backgrounds.

Srihari Yamanoor has over 15 years of experience in the medical device industry. He has worked on new product development and introduction, reliability improvements, manufacturing, and quality. His areas of work include diabetes, women's health, dermatology, cardiology, robotic and conventional diagnostics and surgery, orthopedics, and oncology. He has co-authored three books on applications of the Raspberry Pi family of products in technology, education, hobbies, and other areas. In 2021, Srihari was named one of the Top 100 Healthcare Visionaries by IFAH.

About the Technical Reviewer

Mr. Atonu Ghosh is a PhD research scholar in the Department of Computer Science and Engineering at the Indian Institute of Technology Kharagpur, West Bengal, India. He also has an M.Tech. and a B.Tech. in Computer Science and Engineering. Atonu's research domain includes the Internet of Things (IoT), edge computing, low-power networks, and Industry 4.0. Atonu has built IoT solutions for over nine years and has executed several projects. He is also an active reviewer of research journals and books. Find out more about Atonu or reach him through his personal website https://www.atonughosh.com/.

Acknowledgments

I thank my mother for teaching me the importance of perseverance and patience in life. I am grateful to Nirmal, Spandana, and Kripa at Apress for their kindness and patience during this book's writing and editorial process. I also thank the technical reviewer, Atonu Ghosh, for his valuable feedback in making this book successful. Finally, I thank my friend Balaji Raghavendra for being an inspiration and a sounding board while being stuck with a project.

—Sai Yamanoor

I would like to express my gratitude toward the entire Apress team for their support and patience throughout the writing and editorial process. I also thank my mother, to whom I owe everything, and friends, particularly my Mindshare group of highly qualified professionals from across various fields who have steadfastly encouraged me in various endeavors.

—Srihari Yamanoor

Introduction

Over the past decade, several advances in novel hardware and software solutions have enabled enthusiasts to learn how to prototype, develop, and deploy solutions. The emergence of competing Single-Board Computer (SBC) and microcontroller architectures empowers the development of various combinations of solutions that cater to requirements such as cost, efficiency, form factor, programmability, customizability, and several other factors. Along with these advantages, a key provision is that these tools enable students from various traditional and nontraditional backgrounds to learn essential concepts in multiple fields, including computing, programming, and hardware development, encompassing the integration of sensors, data communication, and display modalities.

The ESP32 family of microcontrollers is well suited for the Internet of Things (IoT) due to its robust computing capabilities, extensive interfacing features, and advanced communication capabilities. There is also the cost compatibility that renders the series of microcontrollers ideal for the democratization of education and deployment worldwide. As a rough estimate, different flavors of ESP32 cost less than $1 (at volume). They can be used for IoT product development in various application areas.

Besides our own work, there is a growing body of specific resources and analogs from similar microcontrollers and SBCs whose project embodiments can be adapted into ESP32-based applications. Lower costs and openness in software and hardware embodiments also make such products ideal for use in and by communities of varying societal needs, including underserved communities in areas including and not limited to healthcare, environmental monitoring, smart wearables, and others.

As enthusiasts of DIY-style education and product development, we are always on the lookout for tools and techniques that are low cost and, wherever possible, open source so that costs do not become a barrier to experiential learning and solution generation. Throughout the chapters, we have selected tools based on these goals, with increasing detail, culminating in the final chapter, which serves as an example for product development. We have thoroughly enjoyed the experience of authoring this book, and we hope you do as well, perusing and building and expanding on our examples to satisfy your own requirements and creativity.

CHAPTER 1

Introduction to the ESP32 Platform

Welcome to *IoT Product Development Using ESP32 Microcontrollers*. Over the following seven chapters, we will explore the ESP32 microcontroller and its use in developing IoT products. We will explore the powerful features of the ESP32 microcontroller with projects such as a weather station, an air quality display, a personal health tracker, and a LoRa sensor node. Our journey culminates in a final project example where we discuss all aspects of IoT product development. Join us on this exciting adventure.

The **Internet of Things** as a concept has been around for a while. It refers to connecting things or objects to the internet to exchange information, such as transmitting sensor data, reporting a machine's status, or receiving commands from a central server. Some examples of early IoT-enabled devices include a PLC system (programmable logic control) connected to the internet through a modem and a soda vending machine at Carnegie Mellon University connected to the local network. This enabled campus members to order their drink of choice remotely.

In recent years, the advent of powerful and low-cost microcontroller families, such as the ESP32 series, has enabled the proliferation of IoT devices in applications such as smartwatches, fitness trackers, smart sensors, and voice/home automation assistants.

In this book, we will explore the powerful features of the ESP32 platform and its applications in developing IoT products, while considering the various aspects of developing IoT hardware. The projects selected are of increasing complexity, from interfacing sensors to the ESP32 to cloud integration. In this chapter, we will kickstart our adventure by familiarizing ourselves with the ESP32 platform, understanding the tools needed for this book's projects, and setting up the required software. We finally discuss the traditional "hello world" example of blinking an LED using the ESP32 microcontroller. Grab a cup of coffee (or any beverage of your choice), and let's get started!

© Sai Yamanoor and Srihari Yamanoor 2025
S. Yamanoor and S. Yamanoor, *IoT Product Development Using ESP32 Microcontrollers*,
https://doi.org/10.1007/979-8-8688-1570-6_1

Introduction to the ESP32 Platform

ESP32 generally refers to a collection of microcontroller families from Espressif Systems, based in Shanghai, China. The microcontrollers are rich in communication interfaces, such as I²C, UART, SPI, and USB, which enable interfacing with sensors to collect data from their surroundings or to stream data through one of these interfaces. They also offer Wi-Fi and/or Bluetooth LE connectivity. The ESP32 family of microcontrollers are especially known for their low cost at low quantities. For example, the ESP32-C3 microcontroller costs US$1, while the ESP32-S3 costs about US$1.85. In order to enable easy integration of ESP32 in IoT products, Espressif offers FCC/CE-certified modules (shown in Figure 1-1) that enable rapid prototyping and easy integration into a product. The pre-certified modules help reduce regulatory certification costs for product developers who don't necessarily have the resources or investments to bring their products to market. You can compare the features of the ESP32 microcontroller variants using this interactive tool: `https://products.espressif.com/#/product-comparison`.

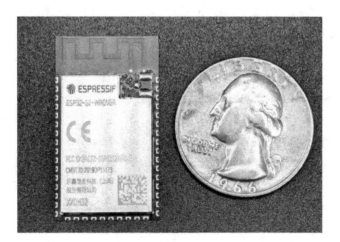

Figure 1-1. *FCC-certified ESP32-S2 module*

ESP32 Microcontroller Variants

In this section, we will discuss the variants of the ESP32 microcontroller. It is not a comprehensive introduction to their features. Still, we will review the options available to someone looking to develop a product with the ESP32. The ESP32 has the following variants:

- The *ESP32* is powered by a 32-bit LX6 Xtensa single or dual-core processor and supports Wi-Fi and Bluetooth protocols.

- The *ESP32-S2* series is powered by a 32-bit LX6 Xtensa single-core processor and supports only Wi-Fi.

- The *ESP32-S3* series is powered by a 32-bit LX7 Xtensa dual-core processor and supports Wi-Fi and Bluetooth protocols.

- The *ESP32-C2* and *ESP32-C3* series are powered by a RISC-V single-core processor and support Wi-Fi and Bluetooth 5.0 protocols.

- The *ESP32-C6* series is powered by a RISC-V single-core processor and supports Wi-Fi, Bluetooth, and Thread/Zigbee protocols.

- The *ESP32-H2* series is also powered by a RISC-V single-core processor that supports Bluetooth LE and Thread/Zigbee protocols.

Note   Apart from the variants discussed above, Espressif also announced the ESP32-P4 series and the ESP32-C5 series. At the time of writing this book, no evaluation tools were available. We recommend checking out the detailed description of each variant at `https://www.espressif.com/en/products/socs`.

Espressif provides a commitment of upwards of ten years to each variant. This means that the individual variant of the ESP32 microcontroller would be in production for the promised duration. The start dates of the longevity commitments for each variant are available here: `https://www.espressif.com/en/products/longevity-commitment`.

The following section will discuss some of the ESP32 microcontroller's features and advantages.

Advantages of the ESP32 Platform

Why choose ESP32? Let's review some of its features and advantages for IoT product development.

1. **Low-cost microcontrollers:** The ESP32 microcontrollers are known for their low cost. For example, as mentioned before, the ESP32-S3 costs about 1.85 USD for a single unit, while the ESP32-C3 microcontroller costs about 1.00 USD. This makes it easier to develop low-cost products using the ESP32.

2. **Module form factor:** Espressif offers modules that simplify the integration of the microcontroller into designs. This includes the RF (Radio Frequency) circuitry for the Wi-Fi/BLE signals, external clock, and input power circuitry. This simplifies the process for those who aren't necessarily familiar with RF-based product development. Figure 1-2 contains three images. On the left is an ESP32-S2 module, which costs about 5.95 USD. In the center is a PCB with an ESP32-S3 module. The right-hand side image shows a PCB with the ESP32-C3 microcontroller. It demonstrates how the use of a module helps eliminate the design complexities.

Figure 1-2. *Comparison of form factor for module vs. microcontroller*

3. **Pre-certified modules:** Any IoT product with a Wi-Fi or Bluetooth radio requires regulatory certification for the market in which it will be sold. For example, radio devices sold in the United States are required to undergo certification to demonstrate that they do not interfere with other devices in their immediate vicinity. The testing requirements depend upon the product's intended use. Espressif sells pre-certified modules that help reduce the burden of testing and certification costs. Figure 1-3 shows a snapshot of the certifications available for the ESP32-S3-WROOM-1 module. In the snapshot, FCC refers to the Federal Communications Commission of the United States, while IC refers to Industry Canada.

Filter	Clear			
Product Series		Found 10 results		Download selected
		Certification	Issue Date	Download
ESP32-H2 Series	+			
ESP32-S2 Series	+	ESP32-S3-WROOM-1 ANATEL Certification	2023.08.04	⭳
ESP32-S3 Series	−			
☐ ESP32-S3		ESP32-S3-WROOM-1 SRRC Certification	2022.06.02	⭳
☑ ESP32-S3-WROOM-1		ESP32-S3-WROOM-1 NCC Certification	2022.05.13	⭳
☐ ESP32-S3-WROOM-1U				
☐ ESP32-S3-WROOM-2		ESP32-S3-WROOM-1 KCC Certification	2022.04.02	⭳
☐ ESP32-S3-MINI-1		ESP32-S3-WROOM-1 IC Certification	2022.01.26	⭳
☐ ESP32-S3-MINI-1U		ESP32-S3-WROOM-1 MIC Certification	2022.01.26	⭳
☐ ESP32-S3-PICO-1				
ESP32-C2 Series	+	ESP32-S3-WROOM-1 Wi-Fi Certification	2022.01.26	⭳
ESP32-C3 Series	+	ESP32-S3 Module BQB Certification	2022.01.26	⭳
ESP32-C6 Series	+			
ESP32-C5 Series	+	ESP32-S3-WROOM-1 CE Certification	2022.01.26	⭳
ESP32 Series	+			
ESP8266 Series	+	ESP32-S3-WROOM-1 FCC Certification	2022.01.26	⭳

Figure 1-3. *List of certifications available for the ESP32-S3-WROOM-1 module*

4. **Development kits:** The ESP32 offers numerous development kits for various applications, including touch screens, wearables, audio applications, and sensor-to-cloud integration. For the uninitiated, a development board helps build prototypes quickly to prove an idea or a concept. Figure 1-4 shows some examples of the available development kits. The board on the left is a development kit in the "Arduino" form factor. The board in the

center is a development board from Adafruit in the "Feather" form factor. The board on the right is an ESP32-S3 development board with a round display. It is suitable for wearable development using the ESP32.

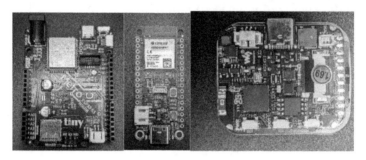

Figure 1-4. *Arduino, Feather, and Wearable form factor developments for ESP32-S3*

5. **Wide user base:** Due to its low cost and extensive development kit availability, the ESP32 is popular among IoT enthusiasts. As a result, it has found its way into various applications, such as home automation and consumer products.

6. **Cloud integration:** The ESP32 supports easy cloud integration through libraries and frameworks from Espressif and popular cloud platform providers. The support enables the transmission of data through various communication protocols to the cloud.

In the next section, we will discuss the development board we will use in this book and the options available to the reader.

This book focuses on product development using the ESP32 microcontroller. From time to time, we recommend add-on hardware, such as sensors, to demonstrate its powerful features. At the beginning of every chapter, we will share the links to the required hardware.

ESP32 Development Board Selection

In this section, we will pick a development board for all the examples and projects discussed in this book. You are welcome to select a development board and module of your choice. Apart from the development board, you also need to purchase some additional components to follow along with the examples discussed in this book. We will provide alternatives to all significant components wherever possible.

If you are unfamiliar with the concept of a development board, it is designed for prototyping electronic components. A development board provides access to all the peripherals available on a microcontroller. It usually also has add-ons like buttons, displays, etc., to aid rapid prototyping. Development boards are typically designed to target specific applications. For example, Figure 1-5 shows an ESP32-S3 development board for wearable applications.

Figure 1-5. *ESP32-S3-based wearable development kit*

ESP32 Module Variant Selection

For this book, we chose the ESP32-S3 module. The ESP32-S3 supports both Wi-Fi and Bluetooth Low Energy (BLE) capabilities. It is suitable for the examples we will discuss in this book. We considered the following factors:

- Low-cost module and development board options

- Programming language options

- Peripherals available for the projects/examples discussed in this book

- Wireless protocols and capabilities generally needed to develop a product

Now that we have chosen the module, we will review the development board options available for the ESP32-S3 module.

ESP32 Development Board Selection

A quick search for an ESP32-S3 module-based development board yields plenty of options. Let's discuss the two most common options and the one we picked for examples discussed in this book.

Adafruit ESP32-S3 Feather

This development board (shown in Figure 1-6) is based on an ESP32-S3-Mini-1 module and is available in the Adafruit Feather form factor. The Adafruit Feather form factor aids rapid prototyping because it is small enough to fit on a breadboard. Adafruit also sells add-on boards called FeatherWings. A FeatherWing board is stackable, and there are FeatherWing boards available for motor controllers, displays, ADCs, sensors, and more. For example, an OLED FeatherWing stacked on top of a Feather board could be used to display sensor data.

The features of the ESP32-S3 Feather include the following:

- Using the ESP32-S3-Mini-1 module enables designing a board using the same module once the concept is proven.

- The board can be powered by a battery or a USB-C cable.

- Battery can be charged via USB-C and includes a LiPo battery monitor.

- Stemma/Qwiic connector enables connecting devices over the I²C interface.

- The sleep current of this board is around 100 uA, and it is suitable for wearable applications.

This dev board costs about 17.50 USD at the time of publication, and it is available from Adafruit (https://www.adafruit.com/product/5477).

Figure 1-6. *Adafruit Feather S3 development board*

The Feather is a standard development board form factor, and other manufacturers sell development boards in this form factor. For example, SparkFun sells the ESP32-S3 Thing Plus (`https://www.sparkfun.com/products/24408`), and Unexpected Maker sells the FeatherS3 (`https://www.adafruit.com/product/5399`).

Adafruit Metro ESP32-S3

This development board comes in the Arduino form factor. It uses the ESP32-S3-WROOM-1 module. Similar to the FeatherWing, an Arduino shield is add-on hardware that enables rapid prototyping. There are tons of Arduino shields available due to the history of Arduinos in DIY electronics. This board costs $24.95, and it is available here: `https://www.adafruit.com/product/5500`.

The features of the Adafruit Metro ESP32-S3 development board (shown in Figure 1-7) are identical to those of the ESP32-S3 Feather except for their form factor and the module used.

Figure 1-7. *Adafruit Metro ESP32-S3 development board*

ESP32-S3-DEVKIT

If you don't have access to the boards discussed above, you can opt for the official development board from Espressif. It is called the ESP32-S3-DEVKITC-1-N8 (shown in Figure 1-8). It uses the same module as the Adafruit Metro, costing about 15 USD. It is available here: https://www.digikey.com/en/products/detail/espressif-systems/ESP32-S3-DEVKITC-1-N8/15199021.

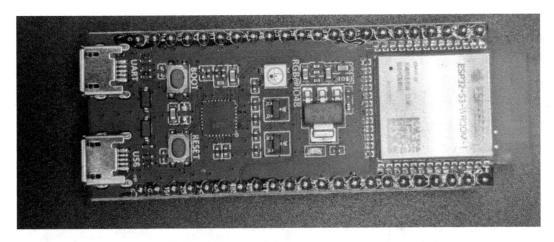

Figure 1-8. *ESP32-S3-DEVKIT*

If you use this development board, you must be prepared to make extensive breadboard connections to your add-on hardware.

Board Selection

Which board should you choose for your prototyping needs? The answer depends on your application type.

1. If unsure of your product's final form factor requirements, we recommend using the Adafruit Metro ESP32-S3. The Metro's Arduino form factor enables easy prototyping with the add-on Arduino shields. The wide-ranging availability of Arduino shields enables building a proof of concept for your product.

2. If you are working on a product that needs to fit into a small enclosure or has a narrow form factor, we recommend opting for the ESP32-S3 Feather.

3. If you are working on a product like a wearable, we recommend using the XIAO ESP32-S3 (shown in Figure 1-9) from Seeed Studio (https://wiki.seeedstudio.com/xiao_esp32s3_getting_started/), which costs 7.49 USD, or the Adafruit QT Py ESP32-S3 (https://www.adafruit.com/product/5426), which costs 12.50 USD. The pins on both development boards are compatible. The

11

board from Seeed Studio is FCC certified. As mentioned earlier, we will discuss the advantages of using an FCC-certified module in the final chapter.

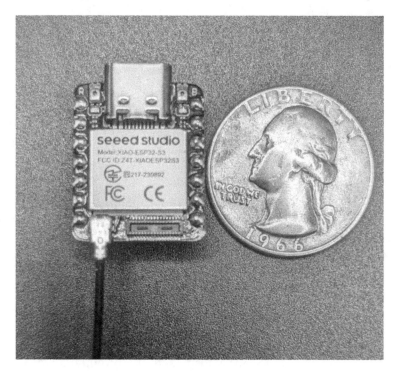

Figure 1-9. *XIAO ESP32-S3 development board*

In this book, we will maintain consistency and use the Adafruit Metro ESP32-S3 for all the projects. We will try to demonstrate the same example using other development boards wherever possible. The code samples discussed in this book should work with any ESP32-S3 development board with minimal changes to the code.

Now that we have selected a development board, we will review its features in the next section.

Tour of the Adafruit Metro ESP32-S3 Development Board

In this section, we will review the features of the development board (Figure 1-10). Each board feature is marked with a red rectangle and a number inside it. The features are described in that numerical order.

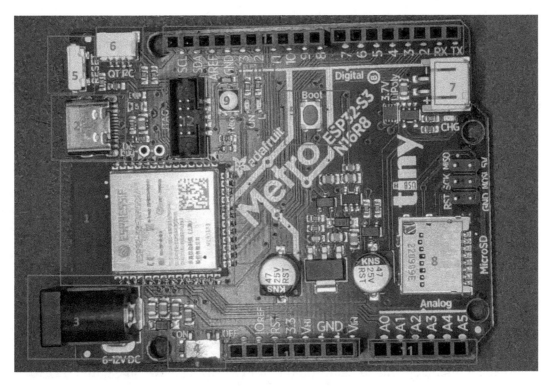

Figure 1-10. *Features of the Adafruit Metro ESP32-S3*

1. As the name of the development board suggests, this board
   is designed around the ESP32-S3-WROOM-1 module. The
   module is FCC certified and can be used in your custom printed
   circuit board design once you prove the concept using the
   development board.

2. USB-C port enables programming the module as well as powering
   the board.

3. The DC power jack enables powering the board using a 6–12V
   power supply.

4. A sliding switch that enables cutting off power to the board.

5. The RESET and BOOT switches enable the module to be reset and
   put into bootloader mode, respectively. We will demonstrate how
   to load firmware onto the module using these two buttons.

6. This is called a Stemma/Qwiic connector. It enables the connection of I²C devices to the board for prototyping purposes. Later chapters will show how to interface sensors using this connector.

7. Connector to interface LiPo batteries and power the module using a battery.

8. MicroSD card slot meant for data logging purposes.

9. Neopixel RGB LED – The user can drive the LED.

10. Red LED and power-on LEDs. The user can control the Red LED. You can cut the power to the power-on LED by cutting the pad on the back of the board.

11. Headers in the Arduino Shield form factor. You can stack add-on hardware using these headers.

12. JTAG header for debugging purposes.

We recommend downloading the pinout from Adafruit (shown in Figure 1-11). It comes in handy while writing code.

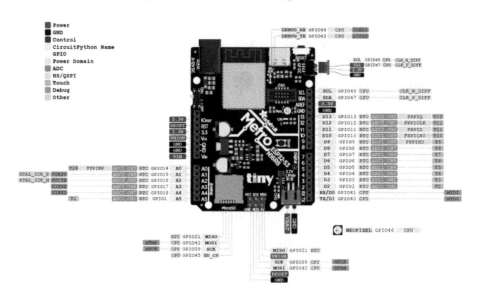

Figure 1-11. *Adafruit Metro ESP32-S3 pinout from Adafruit (License: CC BY-SA 3.0)*

Now that we have reviewed the features of our development board, we will discuss the programming language used in this book.

Programming Language Options and Selection

In this section, we will discuss the programming language options available for the ESP32 microcontrollers. The options include

1. **ESP-IDF:** ESP-IDF refers to Espressif IoT Development Framework. As the name suggests, it is the official SDK (Software Development Kit) from Espressif to build IoT products. The SDK consists of peripheral drivers, libraries, and examples needed to start development using C/C++ programing languages. You can read more about the ESP-IDF here: `https://www.espressif.com/en/products/sdks/esp-idf`.

2. **Arduino:** If you are familiar with programming an Arduino and the Arduino IDE, Espressif provides a Board Support Package and the libraries needed to program in C++ using the Arduino IDE. You can read more about the Arduino Support Package for ESP32 microcontrollers here: `https://docs.espressif.com/projects/arduino-esp32/en/latest/getting_started.html#`.

3. **MicroPython:** In case you are unfamiliar with MicroPython, it is a flavor of the Python programming language designed to program microcontrollers like the ESP32. With MicroPython, it is possible to control the peripherals on the ESP32 from a Python interpreter running on the ESP32. MicroPython offers several advantages:

    a. It offers minimal barrier entry to those who are new to programming since Python is an excellent language for beginners.

    b. MicroPython is a great way to learn embedded hardware programming for those who know Python, as it offers an interpreter running on the microcontroller to interact with the hardware and control the peripherals.

    c. Code written using MicroPython is portable across platforms with minimal code changes. For example, code written for an ESP32-S3 can be easily ported to other variants of ESP32. Code portability is essential to IoT product development because there are scenarios where you might have to switch microcontrollers. These situations include hardware limitations, a particular part going out of production, etc.

d. MicroPython has broad community support. It is an open source project, and the community actively adds support for newer microcontroller variants. At the time of writing this book, ESP32, ESP32-C3, ESP32-S2, and ESP32-S3 variants are supported by MicroPython. You can read about the MicroPython project at `https://micropython.org/`.

4. **CircuitPython:** CircuitPython is a project spun off MicroPython. Adafruit has developed and actively maintained the project. CircuitPython offers the same advantages as MicroPython. Additionally, it offers a storage drive interface. You connect a development board to your computer using a USB cable, and it is enumerated as a flash drive. This enables copying the files needed onto the microcontroller to run your code. Adafruit provides CircuitPython support for almost all popular microcontroller development boards and any add-on hardware they carry in their store. You can read more about CircuitPython at `https://circuitpython.org/`.

Apart from the options discussed above, you can also write code for ESP32 using programming languages like C#, Go, and Rust.

Programming Language Selection

So which language should we choose to get started with IoT product development? In this book, we will use MicroPython for all the projects. It enables us to explain IoT product development with the ESP32 microcontrollers to a broader audience. It also allows us to demonstrate the power of MicroPython by rapidly integrating components like sensors to the ESP32 and the ability to iterate through the design.

The last two chapters will also present examples using the Arduino IDE. Join us on this journey to build products with ESP32 and MicroPython!

If you are comfortable in a programming language other than MicroPython, feel free to use the project examples and adapt it to suit your needs.

Integrated Development Environment Installation

Let's get started by installing the requisite tools for this book.

Thonny IDE

The first step is to install an Integrated Development Environment (IDE) to write code. An IDE helps write, test, and load code ("flashing") onto the ESP32. We recommend installing Thonny IDE. Thonny IDE is an open source IDE available for all operating systems. You can download and install Thonny IDE from here: `https://thonny.org/`.

Download and Install MicroPython Binary

To write code in MicroPython, we need to ensure that we have MicroPython running on the microcontroller. The MicroPython interpreter enables running application scripts to control and interact with the microcontroller's peripherals. The next step is to download the MicroPython binary for our development board. You can download the binaries from the MicroPython downloads page (`https://micropython.org/download/?mcu=esp32s3`). There is no official binary for the module used in the Adafruit Metro ESP32-S3 development board. The module used is the ESP32-S3-WROOM-1-N16R8, which comes with 16 MB of Quad SPI Flash and 16 MB of Octal SPI Flash. The official list of the module variants is shown in Figure 1-12.

Table 1: ESP32-S3-WROOM-1 Series Comparison[1]

Ordering Code[2]	Flash[3, 4]	PSRAM[5]	Ambient Temp.[6] (°C)	Size[7] (mm)
ESP32-S3-WROOM-1-N4	4 MB (Quad SPI)	-	–40 ~ 85	
ESP32-S3-WROOM-1-N8	8 MB (Quad SPI)	-	–40 ~ 85	
ESP32-S3-WROOM-1-N16	16 MB (Quad SPI)	-	–40 ~ 85	18.0
ESP32-S3-WROOM-1-H4	4 MB (Quad SPI)	-	–40 ~ 105	×
ESP32-S3-WROOM-1-N4R2	4 MB (Quad SPI)	2 MB (Quad SPI)	–40 ~ 85	25.5
ESP32-S3-WROOM-1-N8R2	8 MB (Quad SPI)	2 MB (Quad SPI)	–40 ~ 85	×
ESP32-S3-WROOM-1-N16R2	16 MB (Quad SPI)	2 MB (Quad SPI)	–40 ~ 85	3.1
ESP32-S3-WROOM-1-N4R8	4 MB (Quad SPI)	8 MB (Octal SPI)	–40 ~ 65	
ESP32-S3-WROOM-1-N8R8	8 MB (Quad SPI)	8 MB (Octal SPI)	–40 ~ 65	
ESP32-S3-WROOM-1-N16R8	16 MB (Quad SPI)	8 MB (Octal SPI)	–40 ~ 65	
ESP32-S3-WROOM-1-N16R16V[8]	16 MB (Quad SPI)	16 MB (Octal SPI)	–40 ~ 65	

***Figure 1-12.** ESP32-S3-WROOM-1 module variants*

We compiled a binary for running MicroPython on the Adafruit ESP32-S3 Metro development board. You can download the binary from here: `https://github.com/sai-ydev/esp32_s3_binaries`.

MicroPython Installation

Let's discuss how to load the downloaded binary onto the ESP32-S3 module.

Ensure that the board is turned ON for installing MicroPython on to the development board!

---

1. The first step is to connect the development board to a laptop using a USB-C cable. The ESP32-S3 module must be in bootloader mode to load the MicroPython binary. Press and hold the BOOT button while connecting the board using a USB cable, and release the button afterward. This should put your device in bootloader mode. The location of the RESET and BOOT buttons on the development board is shown in Figure 1-10.

2. Alternatively, you can put the development board in bootloader mode after connecting it to the laptop. Press the RESET button once, while you press and hold the BOOT button. Then, you can release the BOOT button.

If your development board becomes unresponsive, you can recover it by loading the MicroPython binary and putting the module into bootloader mode.

3. Launch Thonny IDE and go to Run ➤ Configure interpreter. It should launch a pop-up window, as shown in Figure 1-13.

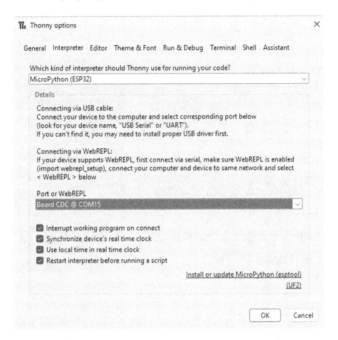

Figure 1-13. *Configure the Micropython interpreter.*

1. The first step is to choose the type of interpreter. Select MicroPython (ESP32).

2. Click Install or update MicroPython (esptool). Select the Target Serial Port as USB JTAG/serial debug unit (as shown in Figure 1-14). From the hamburger button, select the local MicroPython image and load the MicroPython binary you downloaded from the GitHub repository. If you are using a board that comes with official MicroPython support, you need to select the ESP32 series under MicroPython family (ESP32-S3, ESP32-C3, etc.) and choose your board under variant.

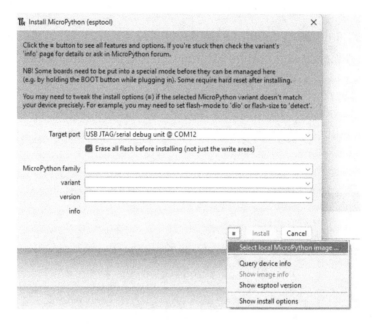

Figure 1-14. Load the MicroPython binary

3. After loading the firmware binary, you should be able to click
   on Install (Figure 1-15).

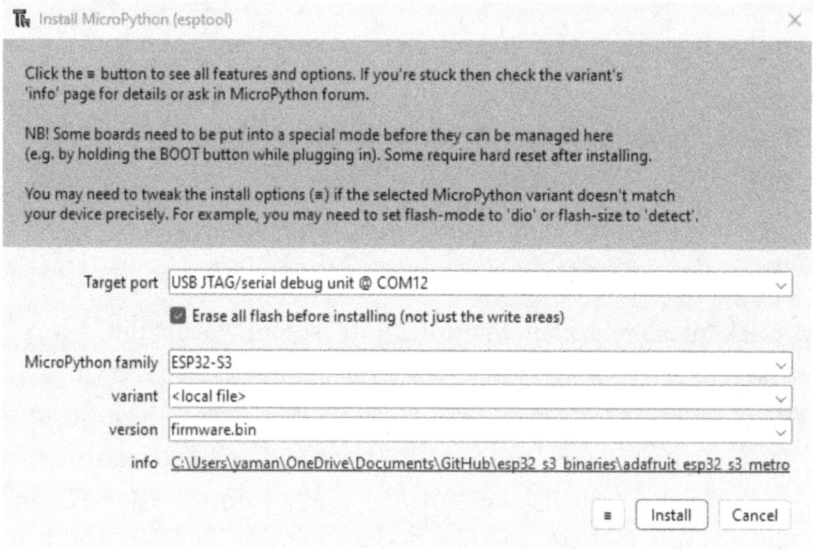

Figure 1-15. Install the MicroPython binary

4. When MicroPython finishes installing, you should see a message, as shown in Figure 1-16.

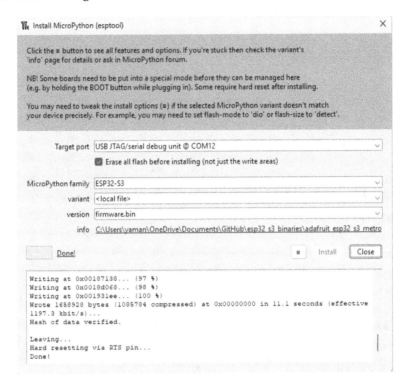

Figure 1-16. *MicroPython finishes installation*

4. Press the RESET button on the development board and close the installation window. On the main window of the Thonny editor, you should see the MicroPython interpreter launched, as shown in Figure 1-17. If you don't see the interpreter, ensure that the ESP32's serial port is selected from the bottom right corner of the window.

Figure 1-17. *MicroPython interpreter*

5. Now that MicroPython is installed, try some basic Python
    arithmetic operations and take it for a test spin! Isn't having a
    flavor of Python running on such a small yet powerful piece of
    hardware exciting?

In the next section, we will install the ESP32 Board Support Package for the Arduino
IDE and write some code to blink LEDs!

Arduino IDE

We recommend installing the Arduino IDE for the Arduino examples discussed in this
chapter. Arduino IDE is also an open source development environment, and it can be
downloaded from here: https://www.arduino.cc/en/software.

Installing ESP32 Board Support Package

After installing the Arduino IDE, we need to install the Board Support Package for the
ESP32 family of microcontrollers.

1. The Board Support Package for the ESP32 platform is available here: `https://espressif.github.io/arduino-esp32/package_esp32_index.json`.

2. Launch the Arduino IDE after installation and go to File ➤ Preferences and select Additional Boards Manager URLs (Figure 1-18).

Figure 1-18. *Select Additional Boards Manager URLs*

3. Save the above URL in the popout window (Figure 1-19).

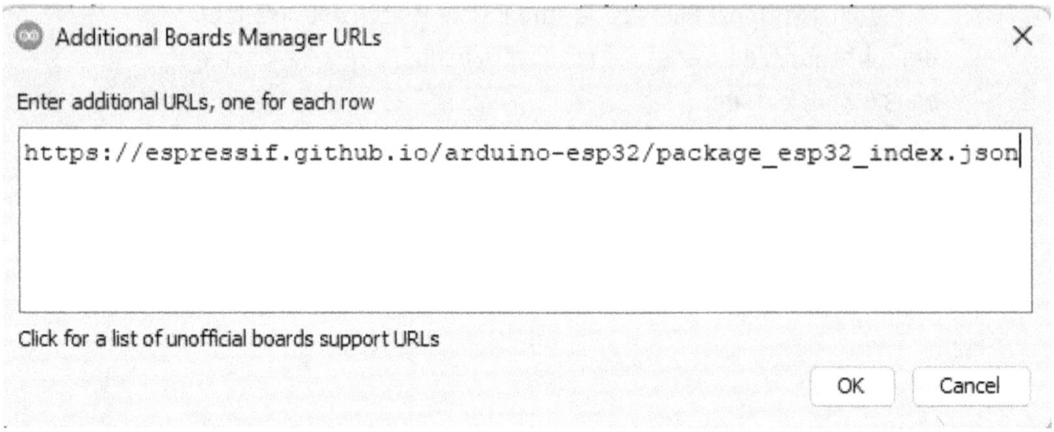

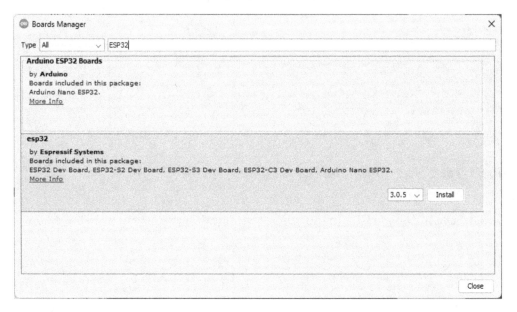

Figure 1-19. *Save the ESP32 Board Support Package URL*

4. Now, go to Tools ➤ Board ➤ Boards Manager. Search
    for ESP32 and install ESP32 by Espressif (Figure 1-20).

Figure 1-20. *Install ESP32 Board Support Package from Espressif Systems*

5. Restart Arduino IDE after the installation is completed.

Now that the ESP32 Board Support Package is installed, we will write some code in
the next section. Onward to the next section!

Documents to Download

We recommend downloading the following documents, as they might be useful as references for the rest of this book. If you choose a different module to follow along with the examples in this book, you must download the equivalent of what we recommend below.

1. **ESP32-S3 Microcontroller Datasheet**: The datasheet is available here: https://www.espressif.com/sites/default/files/documentation/esp32-s3_datasheet_en.pdf.

2. **ESP32-S3-WROOM-1 Datasheet**: The module datasheet is available here: https://www.espressif.com/sites/default/files/documentation/esp32-s3-wroom-1_wroom-1u_datasheet_en.pdf.

3. **Adafruit Metro ESP32-S3 documentation:** We recommend bookmarking the development board documentation (available here: https://learn.adafruit.com/adafruit-metro-esp32-s3/overview) in case you need to refer to the board's pinouts.

4. **Adafruit Metro ESP32-S3 pinout**: The pinout is available here: https://learn.adafruit.com/assets/126034.

In the next section, we will start writing some code in MicroPython.

First Programming Example

In the previous section, we installed Thonny and Arduino IDE and the requisite tools to get started with the ESP32. Now, we will blink an LED in MicroPython.

LED Blinky Using MicroPython

According to the Adafruit Metro ESP32-S3 documentation, an LED is connected to GPIO pin 13 of the development board. We will make it blink at a one-second interval. This code sample is available as *CH01_led_blinky.py* in this book's repository: https://github.com/sai-ydev/IoT_ESP32_Product_Development.

We assume that you have a basic understanding of Python. If you are not that familiar with it, we recommend checking Python programming titles from Apress.

1. The first step is to import the Pin class from the machine module. This enables controlling the ESP32's GPIO pins.

    ```
    from machine import Pin
    ```

2. We need to import the `time` module to inject a one-second delay between turning on and off the LED.

    ```
    import time
    ```

3. We need to declare GPIO pin 13 (declared as BUILTIN_LED) as the output pin. In the code snippet below, we create an led object of the type `Pin` class and as an output pin (`Pin.OUT` parameter in the snippet). In general, LEDs are considered output devices because the microcontroller drives them.

    ```
    BUILTIN_LED = 13

    led = Pin(BUILTIN_LED, Pin.OUT)
    ```

4. We create an infinite loop to toggle the LED on and off at a one-second interval. `while True:` starts a while loop that always tests True and runs indefinitely.

    ```
    while True:
      led.on()
      time.sleep(1)
      led.off()
      time.sleep(1)
    ```

5. In the above snippet, the first line of the indented block (`led.on()`) turns on the LED by setting the GPIO pin 13 to 1. A one-second delay follows this (`time.sleep(1)`).

6. This is followed by turning off the LED (led.off())and another one-second delay.

7. Putting it all together, we have

```
from machine import Pin
import time

BUILTIN_LED = 13

led = Pin(BUILTIN_LED, Pin.OUT)
while True:
  led.on()
  time.sleep(1)
  led.off()
  time.sleep(1)
```

In this section, we used the sleep method to inject delay in terms of seconds. You can use the sleep_ms method to inject delay in terms of milliseconds. For example, sleep_ms(1000) introduces a one-second delay. Refer to the MicroPython documentation to learn more about the time module. You can also learn about the Pin class from the documentation.

8. Type in the above code sample and click the *Run* button in the Thonny IDE (shown in Figure 1-21).

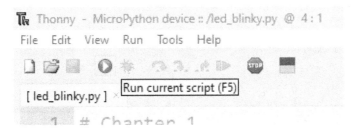

Figure 1-21. *Blinking an LED*

9. The LED should start blinking in a one-second interval
    (Figure 1-22). The LED will stop blinking when you click *Stop* on
    the toolbar.

Figure 1-22. *LED connected to GPIO pin 13 blinking on the ESP32
development board*

10. Thus far, the code runs only when we press Run. What if we want
    to run the script automatically upon turning on the board? In
    the Thonny editor, create a new file called main.py and paste
    the contents of the new file. When you click on *Save*, the editor
    will prompt you to select a location. Select *MicroPython Device*
    (Figure 1-23).

Figure 1-23. *Script saving location*

11. Click on *MicroPython device* and save as *main.py* (Figure 1-24).

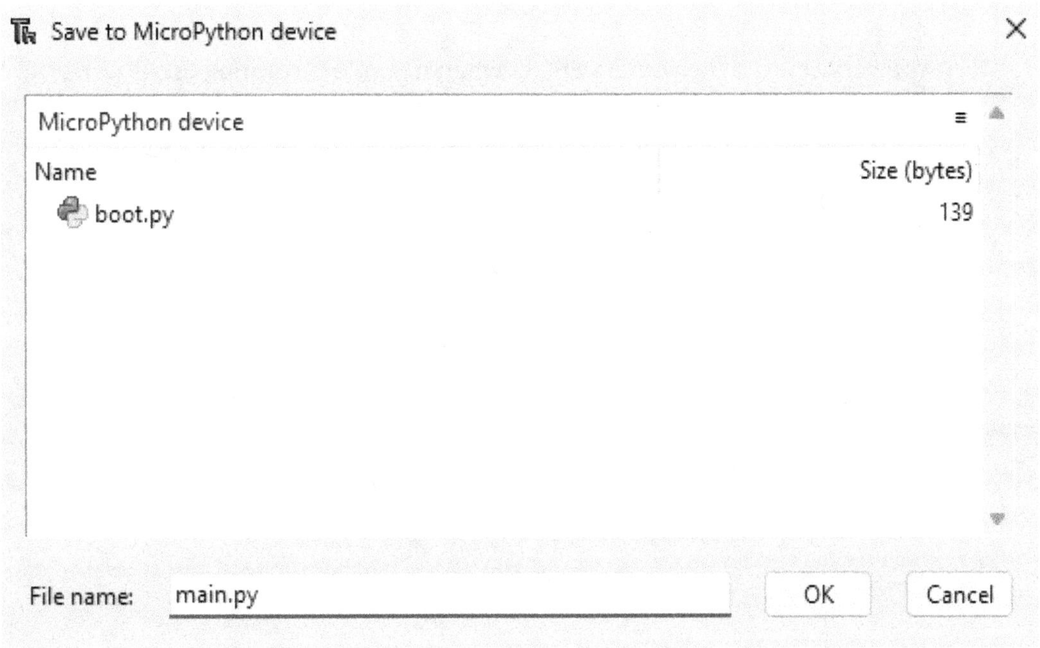

Figure 1-24. *Save as main.py*

12. Now you can run the script on power-up by pressing the RESET button on the development board. Alternatively, you can run the script by pressing the STOP button on the toolbar and pressing CTRL+D from the MicroPython interpreter. CTRL+D performs a soft reboot of the ESP32 (Figure 1-25).

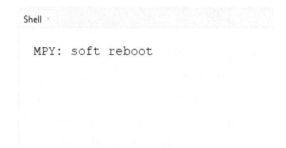

Figure 1-25. *Soft reboot of the ESP32-S3 device*

13. You can view the files on the ESP32 when no code is running on the device. Click Stop and Go to View ➤ Files. This should load the files on the MicroPython device. In Figure 1-26, you will notice two files, namely, boot.py and main.py. The former configures the ESP32 at bootup, and the latter contains the application code. When you save your code as main.py in the ESP32's filesystem, it is executed after bootup. main.py provides a mechanism to automatically execute your application code every time the ESP32 is reset.

Figure 1-26. *Files on the MicroPython device*

14. You can only upload and view files on the ESP32-S3 when no code is actively running on the device. You can interrupt code execution by clicking on Stop.

In this section, we reviewed blinking an LED using MicroPython. The following section will review the same example using the Arduino IDE. If you are not familiar with the Arduino IDE, you can skip ahead to the Wi-Fi example.

LED Blinky Using the Arduino IDE

In this section, we will blink an LED using the Arduino IDE. We assume you have installed the Board Support Package for ESP32 and restarted the Arduino IDE. Let's get started with the LED blinky example!

1. The first step is to set the board by going to Tools ➤ Board ➤ ESP32 Arduino ➤ Adafruit Metro ESP32-S3 (Figure 1-27). This step will work only if you have already installed the ESP32 package with the instructions from the previous section.

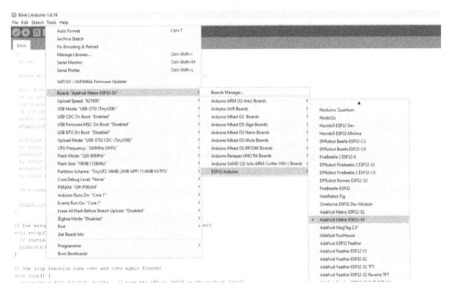

Figure 1-27.   *Set Board to Adafruit Metro ESP32-S3*

2. Then, go to File ➤ Examples ➤ 01. Basics ➤ Blink. This will load the LED Blinking Sketch (Figure 1-28). In the world of Arduino, programs are called *sketches*.

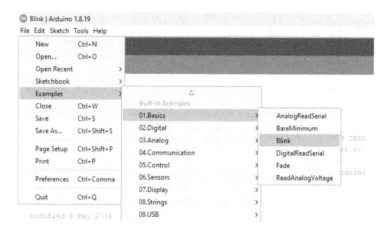

Figure 1-28. *Load the LED blinky example*

3. Let's review the LED Blinking sketch. The first step is the setup function. The setup() function runs once upon reset/power-up. We set up GPIO pin 13 as the output pin in the setup function.

```
void setup() {
  pinMode(LED_BUILTIN, OUTPUT);
}
```

4. The pinMode function sets the pins as either input or output in the above code snippet. The Board Support Package defines the pin connected to the onboard LED as LED_BUILTIN. On most Arduino boards, PIN 13 is defined as the LED pin.

5. The loop() function runs indefinitely. In the loop function, we turn on/off the LED in one-second intervals. In the first line of code, we set the LED_BUILTIN to HIGH to turn on the LED. Then, we introduce a one-second delay by calling the delay function with an argument of 1000 ms.

```
void loop() {
  digitalWrite(LED_BUILTIN, HIGH);
  delay(1000);
  digitalWrite(LED_BUILTIN, LOW);
  delay(1000);
}
```

6. Then, we turn off the LED by setting the pin to LOW and calling the
    delay function with a 1000 ms interval.

7. Next, we must compile and upload the code sample to our board.
    Connect the board to the laptop using a USB cable and make a
    note of the serial port number (this is described in the previous
    section). Set the serial port of the Arduino by going to Tools ➤
    Port ➤ Port Number (as shown in Figure 1-29).

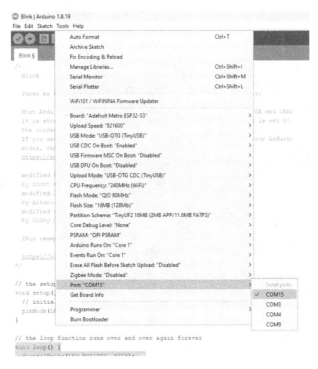

Figure 1-29. *Set the serial port*

8. We can compile and upload the sketch using the Upload button
    (shown in Figure 1-30).

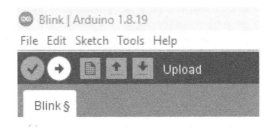

Figure 1-30. *Compile and upload the sketch*

9. The Arduino IDE automatically uploads the sketch upon finishing
    compilation (Figure 1-31). Press the reset button once the
    compiled binary is uploaded, and the onboard LED should start
    blinking at a one-second interval.

If your development board runs MicroPython, the ESP32 must be set in bootloader
mode. To enter bootloader mode, press and hold the BOOT button while pressing
RESET once. This would need to be done only the first time.

```
Done uploading
Writing at 0x0005d0ee... (100 %)
Wrote 333200 bytes (192762 compressed) at 0x00010000 in 2.5 seconds (effective 1082.2 kbit/s)...
Hash of data verified.
Compressed 196176 bytes to 126566...
Writing at 0x00410000... (12 %)
Writing at 0x004180ec... (25 %)
Writing at 0x0042034a... (37 %)
Writing at 0x00425c66... (50 %)
Writing at 0x0042b352... (62 %)
Writing at 0x00430c37... (75 %)
Writing at 0x00435e0f... (87 %)
Writing at 0x0043b816... (100 %)
Wrote 196176 bytes (126566 compressed) at 0x00410000 in 1.4 seconds (effective 1088.6 kbit/s)...
Hash of data verified.

Leaving...
Hard resetting via RTS pin...
```

Figure 1-31. Uploading to the ESP32

Arduino sketches erase the ESP32's memory before uploading a sketch. If you
erased MicroPython for the Arduino example, you can reinstall it by putting the
Arduino in bootloader mode (using the instructions from the previous section).

Now that we have reviewed the LED blinking example using the Arduino IDE, we will
review some Wi-Fi and Bluetooth examples.

Wi-Fi Examples

This section will discuss some Wi-Fi examples to explore the powerful features of the ESP32 microcontroller. The first example scans for Wi-Fi networks and prints their names and signal strength.

From now on, we will discuss our examples only using MicroPython. For Chapters 6 and 7, we will also provide Arduino IDE–based code samples.

Wi-Fi Scanner

The example discussed here is available along with the downloads for this chapter as *ch01_wifi_scanner.py*.

1. The first step is to import the network module to access the Wi-Fi capability.

   ```
   import network
   ```

2. We create a network interface object using the WLAN class from the network module. We specify that we want to create a Wi-Fi client using the network.STA_IF argument. The active method with a True argument activates the network interface.

   ```
   wlan = network.WLAN(network.STA_IF)
   wlan.active(True)
   ```

3. We perform a scan using the scan() method.

   ```
   networks = wlan.scan()
   ```

4. The scan() method returns a list of tuples in the following format: *(ssid, bssid, channel, RSSI, security, hidden)*. We are particularly interested in the network name and its signal strength. We iterate through the list and print each network's name and signal strength.

```
for data in networks:
    name, _, _, rssi, _, _ = data
    decoded_name = name.decode("utf-8")
    print(f"Network: {decoded_name}, S.Strength: {rssi}dBm")
```

5. While unpacking the tuple, we ignore the fields we don't want using a _. The network name is a byte string. We decode it using UTF-8 format and print it to the terminal.

6. Putting it all together, we have

```
import network
```

```
wlan = network.WLAN(network.STA_IF)
wlan.active(True)
networks = wlan.scan()
```

```
for data in networks:
    name, _, _, rssi, _, _ = data
    decoded_name = name.decode("utf-8")
    print(f"Network: {decoded_name}, S.Strength: {rssi}dBm")
```

We get the output shown in Figure 1-32 when we run the above code sample using the *Run Current Script* button from the Thonny editor. The network names have been blanked out for privacy reasons. If your development board is running another program, stop it using the *Stop* button before running this script.

```
>>> %Run -c $EDITOR_CONTENT

MPY: soft reboot
Network: , S.Strength: -25dBm
Network: , S.Strength: -26dBm
Network: , S.Strength: -26dBm
Network: , S.Strength: -42dBm
Network: , S.Strength: -45dBm
Network: , S.Strength: -45dBm
Network: , S.Strength: -46dBm
Network: , S.Strength: -63dBm
Network: , S.Strength: -63dBm
Network: , S.Strength: -64dBm
Network: , S.Strength: -70dBm
Network: , S.Strength: -74dBm
Network: , S.Strength: -85dBm
```

Figure 1-32. *List of networks and their signal strength*

This example was written using the aid of MicroPython's network module documentation. It is available here: https://docs.micropython.org/en/latest/wipy/ tutorial/wlan.html. In the next section, we will connect our ESP32 to the local Wi-Fi.

Connecting to Wi-Fi

In this section, we will test the Wi-Fi connection. This example is identical to the previous one except for a few additions.

1. The first step is to import the network and time modules and initiate an object of the WLAN class. Additionally, we create two variables, ssid and password, which contain the network credentials.

```
import network
import time

ssid = "mywifi"
password = "password"
```

```
wlan = network.WLAN(network.STA_IF)
wlan.active(True)
```

2. We connect to the network using the credentials.

```
wlan.connect(ssid, password)
```

3. We wait until the ESP32 is connected to the Wi-Fi network using a while loop:

```
while not wlan.isconnected():
    print(".")
    time.sleep(1)
```

4. Upon successful connection, we will retrieve the network parameters using the ifconfig method and disconnect from the network.

```
print(f"Success! Connected to {ssid}")
network_params = wlan.ifconfig()

print(f"IP address is {network_params[0]}")

wlan.disconnect()
```

5. Putting it all together, we have

```
import network
import time

ssid = "mywifi"
password = "password"
wlan = network.WLAN(network.STA_IF)
wlan.active(True)

wlan.connect(ssid, password)

while not wlan.isconnected():
    print(".")
    time.sleep(1)
```

```
print(f"Success! Connected to {ssid}")
network_params = wlan.ifconfig()

print(f"IP address is {network_params[0]}")

wlan.disconnect()
```

We get the output shown in Figure 1-33 when we run the above code sample using the *Run Current Script* button from the Thonny editor. If your development board is running another program, stop it using the *Stop* button before running this script.

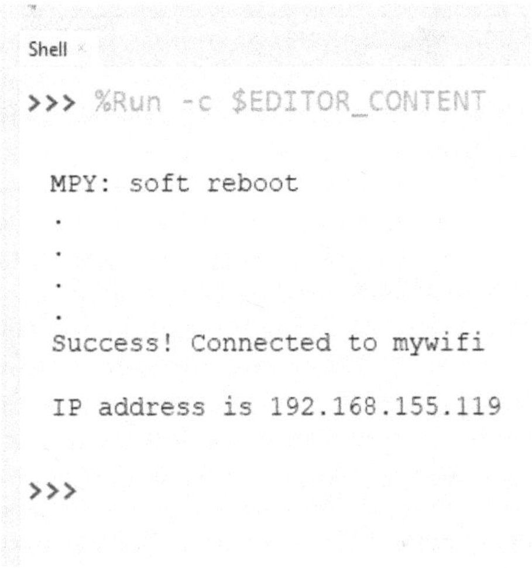

```
Shell

>>> %Run -c $EDITOR_CONTENT

 MPY: soft reboot
   .
   .
   .
   .
 Success! Connected to mywifi

 IP address is 192.168.155.119

>>>
```

Figure 1-33. *Wi-Fi connection*

In this section, we tested the ESP32-S3 module's Wi-Fi capabilities. In the next section, we will test the Bluetooth radio.

Testing ESP32's Bluetooth Capabilities

This section will test the ESP32 module's Bluetooth capabilities by scanning all nearby Bluetooth Low Energy devices. The example discussed in this section is available for download as *ch01_ble_scanner.py*.

Note   Bluetooth Low Energy (BLE) is a vast topic, and we will explore it in depth in Chapter 4. In this section, we will do a simple scan of all nearby devices without delving into detail.

The code sample in this section was developed using the code samples available from the MicroPython repository: `https://github.com/micropython/micropython/blob/master/examples/bluetooth`. The examples are distributed under an MIT license.

1. We get started by importing the requisite modules:

```
import time
import bluetooth
from micropython import const
```

2. We declare the constants used in the script including the scan duration, which is 1000 ms.

```
_IRQ_SCAN_RESULT = const(5)
_IRQ_SCAN_DONE = const(6)
_ADV_TYPE_NAME = const(9)

SCAN_DURATION = 1000
```

3. We declare the functions used to decode the messages. These functions were adopted from the *ble_advertising* example in the MicroPython repository. These functions help with decoding the device name from the incoming scan payload.

```
def decode_field(payload, adv_type):
    i = 0
    result = []
    while i + 1 < len(payload):
        if payload[i + 1] == adv_type:
            result.append(payload[i + 2 : i + payload[i] + 1])
        i += 1 + payload[i]
    return result

def decode_name(payload):
    n = decode_field(payload, _ADV_TYPE_NAME)
    return str(n[0], "utf-8") if n else ""
```

4. Now, we define a method called `irq_callback` that parses the incoming data and events. An `irq` refers to an interrupt request. This callback function is registered with the BLE object to handle all events. It processes _IRQ_SCAN_RESULT and _IRQ_SCAN_ DONE interrupt requests.

```
def irq_callback(event, data):
  if event == _IRQ_SCAN_RESULT:
    _, addr, _, _, ad_data = data
    name = decode_name(ad_data)
    formatted_addr = ":".join(["0x{:02X}".format(i) for i
    in addr])
    print(name, formatted_addr)
  elif event == _IRQ_SCAN_DONE:
    print("Scan Complete")
```

5. Now, we create an object of the BLE class and activate the interface. We also register the `irq_callback` function to handle interrupt requests.

```
ble = bluetooth.BLE()
ble.active(True)
ble.irq(irq_callback)
```

6. We start the scan for peripherals for 1000 ms. We also specify that the scan needs to be performed every 30000 microseconds for 30000 microseconds.

```
ble.gap_scan(SCAN_DURATION, 30000, 30000)
```

7. We wait for at least twice as long to make sure that the scan finishes.

```
# wait for scan to finish
time.sleep_ms(SCAN_DURATION * 2)
```

8.   Putting it all together, we have

```python
import time
import bluetooth
from micropython import const

_IRQ_SCAN_RESULT = const(5)
_IRQ_SCAN_DONE = const(6)
_ADV_TYPE_NAME = const(9)

SCAN_DURATION = 1000

def decode_field(payload, adv_type):
    i = 0
    result = []
    while i + 1 < len(payload):
        if payload[i + 1] == adv_type:
            result.append(payload[i + 2 : i + payload[i] + 1])
        i += 1 + payload[i]
    return result

def decode_name(payload):
    n = decode_field(payload, _ADV_TYPE_NAME)
    return str(n[0], "utf-8") if n else ""

def irq_callback(event, data):
  if event == _IRQ_SCAN_RESULT:
    _, addr, _, _, ad_data = data
    name = decode_name(ad_data)
    formatted_addr = ":".join(["0x{:02X}".format(i) for i
    in addr])
    print(name, formatted_addr)
  elif event == _IRQ_SCAN_DONE:
    print("Scan Complete")
```

```
ble = bluetooth.BLE()
ble.active(True)
ble.irq(irq_callback)
ble.gap_scan(SCAN_DURATION, 30000, 30000)
# wait for scan to finish
time.sleep_ms(SCAN_DURATION * 2)
```

We get the output shown in Figure 1-34 when we run the above code sample using the *Run Current Script* button from the Thonny editor. If your development board is running another program, stop it using the *Stop* button before running this script.

```
Shell ×
    0xF3:0xB1:0xD5:0xB2:
    0x21:0x63:0xA6:0xF4:
    0x21:0x63:0xA6:0xF4:
    0x78:0x9C:0x85:0x06:
    0x55:0x40:0xC5:0x14:
    0x21:0x63:0xA6:0xF4:
  Philips Sonicare 0x24:0xE5:0xAA:
    0x6A:0xDB:0x59:0xE
  Philips Sonicare 0x24:0xE5:0xAA:
    0x55:0x40:0xC5:
    0x21:0x63:0xA6:
    0x78:0x9C:0x85:
    0x21:0x63:0xA6:
    0x6B:0x41:0xA4:
    0x5C:0x94:0x53:
    0x21:0x63:0xA6:
  Scan Complete
```

Figure 1-34. *BLE scanner results*

In Figure 1-34, you will notice the device addresses and names of the BLE devices for which one is available. For example, the ESP32 has retrieved the name and address of an electric toothbrush.

Conclusion

In this chapter, we started with the ESP32 microcontroller and its variants. We selected the ESP32-S3 variant for this book. We reviewed the development board options available for the ESP32-S3 and selected one for the examples discussed in this chapter. We also tested the development board by taking it for a spin with three simple examples. The next chapter will review the process of building a weather station using the ESP32. Onward to Chapter 2!

CHAPTER 2

Building a Weather Station

Welcome to Chapter 2. We hope you are excited to join us in building products using the ESP32. In this chapter, we will discuss the most discussed topic, the weather, and how you can build IoT product prototypes that interact with sensors and other elements of the IoT ecosystem.

Description

This chapter will integrate an off-the-shelf weather station into the Adafruit Metro ESP32-S3. The intent is to demonstrate the ease of integrating sensors with the ESP32-S3 microcontroller and publishing the sensor data to the cloud with a simple example. Your dashboard should look like the one shown in Figure 2-1.

© Sai Yamanoor and Srihari Yamanoor 2025
S. Yamanoor and S. Yamanoor, *IoT Product Development Using ESP32 Microcontrollers*,
https://doi.org/10.1007/979-8-8688-1570-6_2

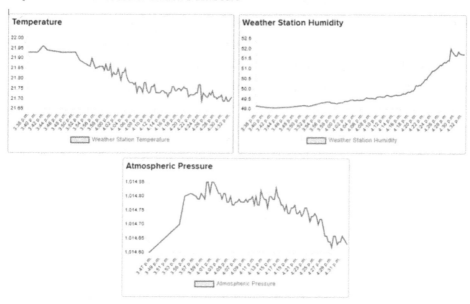

Figure 2-1. *Weather station interfaced to the Adafruit ESP32-S3 and the Weather Station Dashboard displaying Temperature, Humidity and Atmospheric Pressure Data*

Components Used in This Project

For this project, you need an Adafruit ESP32-S3 development kit. You also need weather sensors of your choice. Table 2-1 lists the components needed for this chapter.

Table 2-1. *Components used in this chapter*

Item	Description	Price (in USD)	Link
1	Adafruit Metro ESP32-S3	24.95	https://www.adafruit.com/product/5500
2	Weather sensors	Cost varies based on the sensor	See discussion below

Use Case

Why are we discussing a weather station as an example? Let's consider the following scenario. You have been tasked with developing a product that will be installed at your customer's location. Your customer has sites across the country. Your product interfaces with sensors that collect and upload data from its environment to the cloud. The data uploaded provides analytics to your customers or replenishes a product your company sells. You are responsible for designing a product deployed as a large fleet that uploads its data to the cloud. We wanted to show how to build a prototype for such an application using off-the-shelf hardware. It can be any sensor, but we demonstrated it with a weather station kit. While you work through this chapter, please consider how to scale this prototype into a fleet.

Weather Sensor Selection

You are welcome to choose any sensor, but if you are looking for a weather station, follow the example discussed in this chapter. They are

1. **Lark Weather Station:** The Lark Weather Station costs 150 USD and is available here: https://www.dfrobot.com/product-2785. html. While the Lark Weather Station is expensive, it has a rugged build and comes with mounts for outdoor use. It can report wind speed, direction, temperature, humidity, and atmospheric

pressure. Using the connectors available on board, other sensors can also be integrated. This is the weather station we chose for this chapter. The portable kit comes with a tripod mount for installation.

2. **SparkFun Weather Meter Kit:** The SparkFun Weather Meter Kit costs 80 USD and is available here: `https://www.sparkfun.com/products/15901`. This kit has a rain gauge, anemometers, and a wind direction vane. We are reluctant to recommend this sensor because the add-on hardware (Link: `https://www.sparkfun.com/products/13956`) needed to interface this weather kit is out of stock at the time of writing this chapter. If you can build your prototyping tool, you need a couple of RJ11 connectors soldered onto a prototyping board.

3. **Adafruit Anemometer Kit:** The Adafruit Anemometer Kit costs 45 USD and is available here: `https://www.adafruit.com/product/1733`. This kit only comes with a wind speed sensor and is unsuitable for outdoor use.

You don't necessarily need a weather station kit for the project discussed in this chapter. You can adapt the code sample discussed in this chapter to any sensor of your choice.

Sensor Integration

Let's start by integrating the sensor to the ESP32-S3 on the Adafruit Metro Development Board. The weather station comes with an I²C and UART communication interface. In this chapter, we will use the UART interface and discuss the I²C interface in the next chapter.

Introduction to the UART Interface

The UART interface refers to the **U**niversal **A**synchronous **R**eceiver **T**ransmitter. The word asynchronous refers to the clock of a reference clock source. It is meant to communicate between a sensor and an MCU using a transmitter (TX) and a receiver (RX) pin. The transmitter and the receiver of the MCU and the sensor are interconnected, as shown in Figure 2-2.

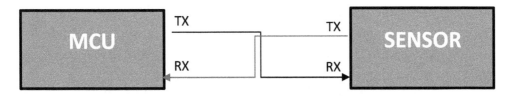

Figure 2-2. *Schematic representation of UART connection between a sensor and an MCU*

The MCU and the sensor are configured to transmit at a speed known as the baud rate. The Lark Weather Station is configured to run at 115200 bits per second. Apart from the baud rate, UART interfaces require additional configuration, such as the number of stop bits and parity checking. For example, 115200 8N1 refers to a 115200 baud rate, 8 bits per data frame, no parity checking, and one stop bit. Each data frame of a UART transmission consists of a start bit, 8 data bits, and a stop bit. Parity checking refers to checking for errors in noisy environments. UART interfaces are meant to talk to one sensor at a time. You can read about UART interfaces at `https://learn.sparkfun.com/ tutorials/serial-communication/serial-intro`.

Setting Up the UART Interface

Since the weather station kit can communicate via I²C or UART interface, we will configure the station to operate via UART. When the weather station is plugged into a computer using a USB-C cable, it is enumerated as a USB storage device. In the contents of the storage device, the file *config.txt* needs to be configured as follows:

```
Communication:UART
Sample_Rate:30 S
Record:OFF
Delay_Record:10
Light_Switch:OFF
Low_Power:OFF
```

A four-pin connector next to the USB-C connector enables the weather station to be connected to a microcontroller. Now, we can connect the sensor to the Adafruit Metro ESP32-S3 using a four-pin JST connector (which comes with the kit) as shown in Table 2-2.

Table 2-2. *Pinouts for interfacing the weather station to the Adafruit Metro ESP32-S3*

Sensor Pin	Adafruit Metro ESP32-S3 Pin
Red (3.3V)	3.3V
Black (GND)	GND
Blue (RX)	D5 (TX)
Green (TX)	D4 (RX)

Next, we will take the sensor for a spin using the driver available from the manufacturer.

Testing the Weather Station Kit

Let's take the weather station for a spin to ensure the connections work. The Python drivers for the weather station are available under an MIT license here: `https://gitee.com/liliang9693/ext-yunque/blob/master/python/libraries/DFRobot_Atmospherlum.py`.

We made some modifications to work in MicroPython. As mentioned in Chapter 1, the most significant advantage of MicroPython is that it can easily port Python code to MicroPython. The modified MicroPython driver is available for download along with this chapter as *dfrobot_weatherstation.py*.

We have observed some bugs in the Python library provided by the manufacturer and fixed most of them. We recommend using the drivers we have made available for download along with this chapter.

Let's take a look at the code sample to test the weather station kit:

1. The first step is importing the UART class from the `machine` library of MicroPython.

   ```
   from machine import UART
   ```

2. The next step is importing the `DFRobot_Atmospherlum_UART` class from `dfrobot_weatherstation.py` and the `utime` library for delays.

   ```
   from dfrobot_weatherstation import DFRobot_Atmospherlum_UART
   import utime
   ```

3. The ESP32-S3 microcontroller has three UART ports, namely, ports 0, 1, and 2. We will be using UART port 1 for this example. We initialize the UART interface 1 at 115200 baud rate and set GPIO pin 5 as the TX pin and GPIO pin 4 as the RX pin.

   ```
   uart1 = UART(1, baudrate=115200, tx=5, rx=4)
   ```

4. We initialize the `DFRobot_Atmospherlum_UART` class by passing the `uart1` object.

   ```
   weather_sensor = DFRobot_Atmospherlum_UART(uart1)
   ```

5. Now, we can collect data from the weather station in an infinite loop in one-second intervals. The `get_information` method returns all sensor data, including temperature, humidity, atmospheric pressure, wind speed, and direction.

   ```
   while True:
       print(weather_sensor.get_information(True))
       utime.sleep(1)
   ```

6. Alternatively, the individual parameters can be retrieved using the `get_value` method, and their corresponding units can be retrieved using the `get_unit` method. Both methods take the parameter name as a string argument. According to the documentation, the string names of the sensors are `Temp`, `Humi`, `Pressure`, `Speed`, and `Dir`. We will use these parameters to retrieve the corresponding sensor data in the next example.

7. Putting all together, we have

```python
from machine import UART
from dfrobot_weatherstation import DFRobot_Atmospherlum_UART
import utime

uart1 = UART(1, baudrate=115200, tx=5, rx=4)
weather_sensor = DFRobot_Atmospherlum_UART(uart1)

while True:
    print(weather_sensor.get_information(True))
    utime.sleep(1)
```

You can type in the above code sample and run it using the *Run Current Script* button from the Thonny editor (Figure 2-3).

Figure 2-3. *Run Current Script button*

The output similar to Figure 2-4 is observed where the sensor data is printed to the terminal at a one-second interval. The windspeed is zero because the weather station was indoors at the time of writing this chapter.

```
Shell
2010_00_02_19:43:25, WindSpeed:0.0 m/s, WindDirection:N, Altitude:-0.60 m, Pressure:1015.04 hPa, Temp:22.42 C, Humi:49.51 %RH
2010_00_02_19:43:25, WindSpeed:0.0 m/s, WindDirection:N, Altitude:-0.60 m, Pressure:1015.04 hPa, Temp:22.42 C, Humi:49.51 %RH
2010_00_02_19:43:25, WindSpeed:0.0 m/s, WindDirection:N, Altitude:-0.60 m, Pressure:1015.04 hPa, Temp:22.42 C, Humi:49.51 %RH
2010_00_02_19:43:25, WindSpeed:0.0 m/s, WindDirection:N, Altitude:-0.60 m, Pressure:1015.04 hPa, Temp:22.42 C, Humi:49.51 %RH
2010_00_02_19:43:55, WindSpeed:0.0 m/s, WindDirection:N, Altitude:-0.38 m, Pressure:1015.07 hPa, Temp:22.44 C, Humi:49.46 %RH
2010_00_02_19:43:55, WindSpeed:0.0 m/s, WindDirection:N, Altitude:-0.38 m, Pressure:1015.07 hPa, Temp:22.44 C, Humi:49.46 %RH
2010_00_02_19:43:55, WindSpeed:0.0 m/s, WindDirection:N, Altitude:-0.38 m, Pressure:1015.07 hPa, Temp:22.44 C, Humi:49.46 %RH
2010_00_02_19:43:55, WindSpeed:0.0 m/s, WindDirection:N, Altitude:-0.38 m, Pressure:1015.07 hPa, Temp:22.44 C, Humi:49.46 %RH
2010_00_02_19:43:55, WindSpeed:0.0 m/s, WindDirection:N, Altitude:-0.38 m, Pressure:1015.07 hPa, Temp:22.44 C, Humi:49.46 %RH
2010_00_02_19:43:55, WindSpeed:0.0 m/s, WindDirection:N, Altitude:-0.38 m, Pressure:1015.07 hPa, Temp:22.44 C, Humi:49.46 %RH
2010_00_02_19:43:55, WindSpeed:0.0 m/s, WindDirection:N, Altitude:-0.38 m, Pressure:1015.07 hPa, Temp:22.44 C, Humi:49.46 %RH
2010_00_02_19:43:55, WindSpeed:0.0 m/s, WindDirection:N, Altitude:-0.38 m, Pressure:1015.07 hPa, Temp:22.44 C, Humi:49.46 %RH
2010_00_02_19:43:55, WindSpeed:0.0 m/s, WindDirection:N, Altitude:-0.38 m, Pressure:1015.07 hPa, Temp:22.44 C, Humi:49.46 %RH
2010_00_02_19:43:55, WindSpeed:0.0 m/s, WindDirection:N, Altitude:-0.38 m, Pressure:1015.07 hPa, Temp:22.44 C, Humi:49.46 %RH
2010_00_02_19:43:55, WindSpeed:0.0 m/s, WindDirection:N, Altitude:-0.38 m, Pressure:1015.07 hPa, Temp:22.44 C, Humi:49.46 %RH
2010_00_02_19:43:55, WindSpeed:0.0 m/s, WindDirection:N, Altitude:-0.38 m, Pressure:1015.07 hPa, Temp:22.44 C, Humi:49.46 %RH
2010_00_02_19:43:55, WindSpeed:0.0 m/s, WindDirection:N, Altitude:-0.38 m, Pressure:1015.07 hPa, Temp:22.44 C, Humi:49.46 %RH
2010_00_02_19:43:55, WindSpeed:0.0 m/s, WindDirection:N, Altitude:-0.38 m, Pressure:1015.07 hPa, Temp:22.44 C, Humi:49.46 %RH
```

Figure 2-4. *Weather station data*

Now that we know the sensor works, we must build a dashboard to publish our data.

Publishing Data to the Cloud

In this section, we will discuss publishing our data to the cloud. We will use Adafruit IO, a free basic service from Adafruit (https://io.adafruit.com/). We recommend signing up for a free account.

We will build a dashboard to publish temperature, humidity, and atmospheric pressure data to the cloud.

After creating an account, we recommend creating three feeds for the three sensors, as shown in Figure 2-5. The feeds can be created by clicking *New Feed* under the Feeds tab.

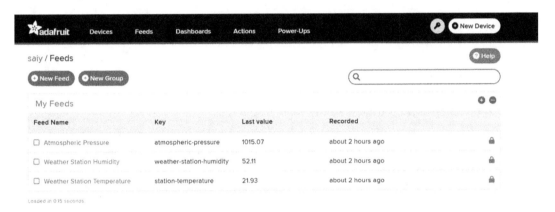

Figure 2-5. *Create feeds for sensors*

We need to create a webhook URL for each feed. You can locate the webhooks generator when you click on a feed name. They are located toward the bottom right, as shown in Figure 2-6. Webhooks enable us to publish data from the ESP32-S3.

Figure 2-6. *Locate webhooks on the feed page*

When you click on webhooks, a create option is available at the bottom of the pop-up window (Figure 2-7).

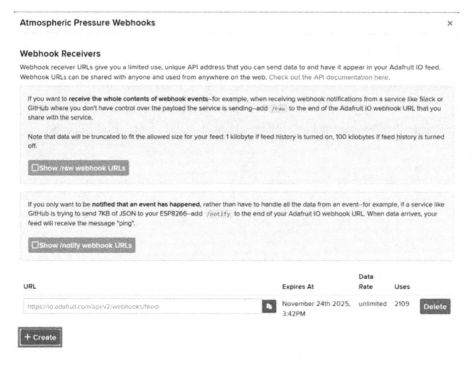

Figure 2-7. *Create webhooks*

While creating the webhook, set the expiration to a year and set the data rate limit to 5 per minute (Figure 2-8). The data rate limit refers to the number of requests your product can make in a minute. This prevents your code from erroneously making multiple requests to the webhook URL.

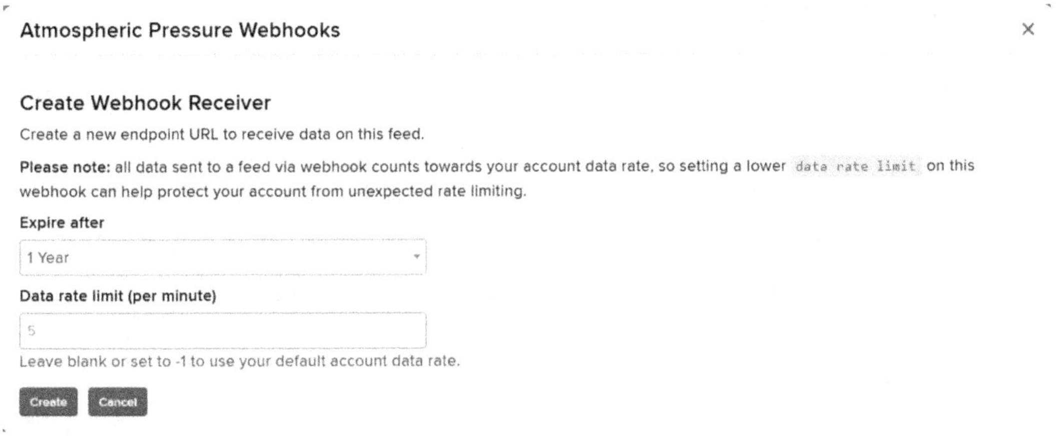

Figure 2-8. *Set data rate limit and expiration date*

Figure 2-9 shows a webhook created with a one-year expiration date and a data rate limit of 5 requests per minute. After creating the webhook, save the URL to use in the MicroPython code sample. You have to repeat this for all three feeds.

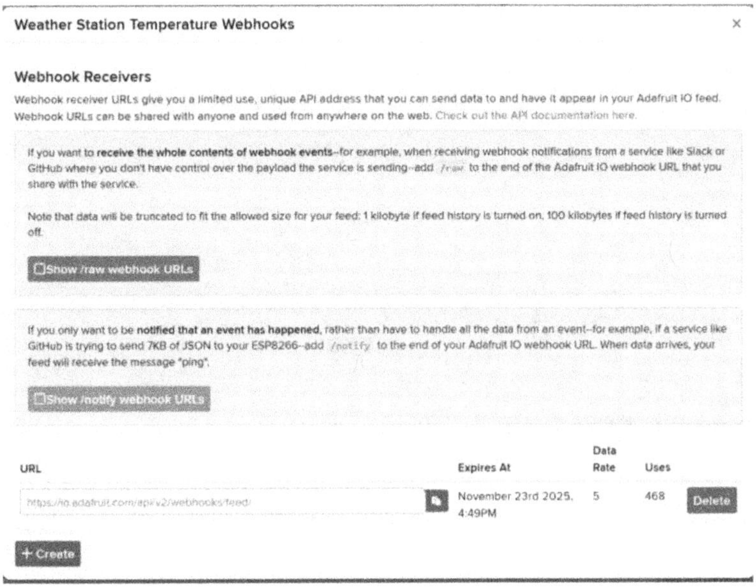

Figure 2-9. *Creating webhook URL*

Before we jump into our code sample, we need to create and save a file called secrets. py that saves your Wi-Fi credentials on the ESP32-S3 memory. This makes it easier to share requisite credentials across code samples.

Creating secrets.py

In Thonny IDE, let's create a new file called secrets.py. We will store three variables, namely:

```
SSID = "MyWifi"
PASSWORD = "Password"
```

The SSID and PASSWORD refer to the credentials of your local Wi-Fi network.

1. We will upload this sample code to the device. In the Thonny IDE, make sure that you view the file directory. This can be accomplished by going to View ➤ Files (Figure 2-10).

Figure 2-10. *Enable File Viewer in Thonny IDE*

2. At the top is the file directory of your computer. At the bottom is the file system of the Adafruit Metro ESP32-S3. We are going to upload this file to the MicroPython device.

3. Before we upload the file, we need to ensure that no active program is running on the device. You can stop it by using the STOP button on the toolbar (Figure 2-11). If this doesn't work, you can select the shell window at the bottom of the IDE and press *CTRL+C.*

Figure 2-11. *Stop programs using the STOP button*

4. Right-click on *secrets.py* located in your local directory and select *Upload to /* (Figure 2-12).

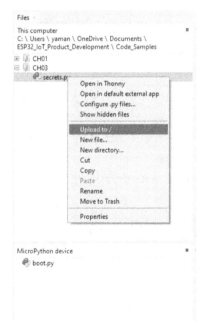

Figure 2-12. *Right-click and upload secrets.py*

5. This should upload secrets.py to our device and be visible in its file directory (as shown in Figure 2-13).

Figure 2-13. *secrets.py uploaded to Adafruit Metro ESP32-S3*

6. Now, we can use *secrets.py*, which contains the requisite credentials for other code samples. This also helps us avoid uploading our private credentials to a public code repository. You can ignore *secrets.py* when setting up your repository.

Publishing Data Using Webhooks

Now, we will review the code required to publish data to the Adafruit IO Feed. This code sample is available for download along with this chapter as *weather_station_publish.py*.

1. The first step is importing the libraries needed for our code. This includes urequests to make a POST request to the Adafruit IO server, network library to connect to the Wi-Fi network, secrets. py for the credentials, UART class, and the DFRobot_Atmospherlum_ UART class for the weather station communications.

```
import urequests
import network
import utime
```

```
import secrets
from machine import UART
from dfrobot_weatherstation import DFRobot_Atmospherlum_UART
```

2. We define a list called PARAMS that contains all the string parameters we will use as arguments when we call the get_value method of the DFRobot_Atmospherlum_UART class. We are going to query the weather station for data from three sensors, namely, temperature, humidity, and pressure.

```
PARAMS = ["Temp", "Humi", "Pressure"]
```

3. The webhook URL saved after creating a webhook in the previous section looks something like this: https://io.adafruit.com/ api/v2/webhooks/feed/abcdefghijk123456789

4. The information after feed/ is your feed ID. So *abcdefghijk123456789* is an example of a feed ID.

5. We define another list called FEED_ID, which contains the feed IDs for all the webhook URLs created in the previous section.

6. The information in the snippet below has been modified for privacy reasons. You must include your actual URL.

```
FEED_ID = [
    "Feed1IDhere",
    "Feed2IDhere",
    "Feed3IDhere"
]
```

7. We create a dictionary called parameters, which contains all the information that will be appended to the URL when making the POST request to the Adafruit IO server.

```
parameters = {
    "Content-Type" : "application/json",
}
```

8. We initialize the UART interface and the weather sensor library.

```
uart = UART(1, baudrate=115200, tx=5, rx=4)
weather_sensor = DFRobot_Atmospherlum_UART(uart)
```

9. Now, we are ready to connect to the Wi-Fi and print the IP address of our local network. Pay attention to the use of secrets.py to retrieve our network credentials.

```
wlan = network.WLAN(network.STA_IF)
wlan.active(True)
wlan.connect(secrets.SSID, secrets.PASSWORD)

while not wlan.isconnected():
    print(".")
    utime.sleep(1)

print(f"Success! Connected to {secrets.SSID}")
network_params = wlan.ifconfig()
print(f"IP address is {network_params[0]}")
```

10. Next, we define a function called post_id that makes the POST request to upload the data to the Adafruit IO server using the webhook URL. Before we make the request, we append all the parameters to the URL using & between each parameter. The parameters appended include the data format (JSON) and the value we want to upload to the server. The parameters are appended in the "<field>=<value>" format. We recommend printing the URL to understand the parameters appended.

```
def post_id(feed_id, data):
    url = 'https://io.adafruit.com/api/v2/webhooks/feed/'
    url += feed_id + "/?"
    for key, value in parameters.items():
        url += key + "=" + value + "&"
    url += "value=" + data

    try:
        response = urequests.post(url)
```

```
except Exception as error:
    print(error)
else:
    if response.status_code == 200:
        print(response.json())
    else:
        print(response.reason)
```

11. Next, we define the `main` function, which includes an infinite `while` loop where we iterate through the `PARAMS` list. We use the `get_value` method of the weather sensor library for each parameter in the list to query for the sensor data. Then, we use the `post_id` function defined earlier to upload the sensor data to the server. We make use of the feed ID corresponding to the sensor. We inject a 15-second delay between consecutive queries to avoid exceeding the five requests per minute limit we set for the webhook URLs.

```
def main():
    while True:
        for idx, param in enumerate(PARAMS):
            data = weather_sensor.get_value(param)
            post_id(FEED_ID[idx], data)
            utime.sleep(1)
            print("-------------------------")
        utime.sleep(15)

if __name__ == "__main__":
    main()
```

Putting it all together, we have

```
import urequests
import network
import utime
import secrets
from machine import UART
from dfrobot_weatherstation import DFRobot_Atmospherlum_UART
```

```python
PARAMS = ["Temp", "Humi", "Pressure"]
FEED_ID = [
    "Feed1IDhere",
    "Feed2IDhere",
    "Feed3IDhere"
]

parameters = {
    "Content-Type" : "application/json",
}

uart = UART(1, baudrate=115200, tx=5, rx=4)
weather_sensor = DFRobot_Atmospherlum_UART(uart)

wlan = network.WLAN(network.STA_IF)
wlan.active(True)
wlan.connect(secrets.SSID, secrets.PASSWORD)

while not wlan.isconnected():
    print(".")
    utime.sleep(1)

print(f"Success! Connected to {secrets.SSID}")
network_params = wlan.ifconfig()
print(f"IP address is {network_params[0]}")

def post_id(feed_id, data):
    url = 'https://io.adafruit.com/api/v2/webhooks/feed/'
    url += feed_id + "/?"
    for key, value in parameters.items():
        url += key + "=" + value + "&"
    url += "value=" + data

    try:
        response = urequests.post(url)
    except Exception as error:
        print(error)
```

```
    else:
        if response.status_code == 200:
            print(response.json())
        else:
            print(response.reason)

def main():
    while True:
        for idx, param in enumerate(PARAMS):
            data = weather_sensor.get_value(param)
            post_id(FEED_ID[idx], data)
            utime.sleep(1)
            print("------------------------")
        utime.sleep(15)

if __name__ == "__main__":
    main()
```

You can type in the above code sample and run it using the *Run Current Script* button from the Thonny editor (Figure 2-14).

Figure 2-14. *Run Current Script button*

The output is similar to Figure 2-15, where the data is uploaded to the Adafruit IO server every 15 seconds.

MPY: soft reboot
Success! Connected to
IP address is 192.168.1.77
{'created_at': '2024-11-25T08:20:38Z', 'id':   , 'expiration': '2024-12-25T08:20:38Z', 'created_epoch': 1732522838, 'feed_id': 2943536, 'v
alue': '22.07', 'feed_key': 'station-temperature'}

{'created_at': '2024-11-25T08:20:40Z', 'id':   , 'expiration': '2024-12-25T08:20:40Z', 'created_epoch': 1732522840, 'feed_id': 2944001, 'v
alue': '51.76', 'feed_key': 'weather-station-humidity'}

{'created_at': '2024-11-25T08:20:44Z', 'id':   , 'expiration': '2024-12-25T08:20:44Z', 'created_epoch': 1732522844, 'feed_id': 2944002, 'v
alue': '1015.04', 'feed_key': 'atmospheric-pressure'}

MicroPython (ESP32) • Board CDC @ COM15 x

Figure 2-15. *Uploading data to the Adafruit IO server*

We can view the data in our Adafruit IO account, as shown in Figure 2-16, which shows the temperature data uploaded using the ESP32-S3 microcontroller. You must be able to view the data feed for all three sensor streams.

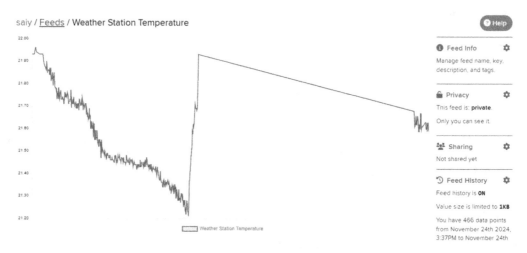

Figure 2-16. *Temperature data uploaded to the Adafruit IO server*

Now that we are uploading data to the cloud, we will review setting up a dashboard for all three sensor streams.

Dashboard Setup

Let's review setting up a dashboard where we can view all three sensor streams on a dashboard. Your account has a Dashboards tab to create a new dashboard to review your sensor data streams (Figure 2-17).

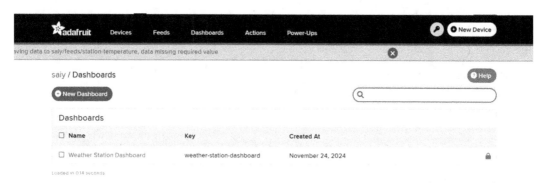

Figure 2-17. *Create a new dashboard*

Select Create New Block under Dashboard Settings in your new dashboard, as shown in Figure 2-18.

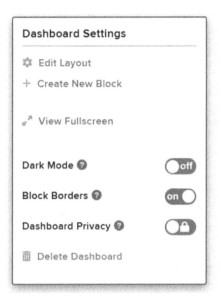

Figure 2-18. *Create New Block*

Select a line chart as shown in Figure 2-19.

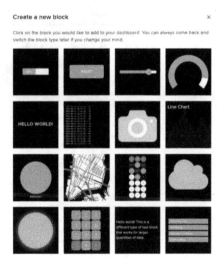

Figure 2-19. *Select a line chart*

Select a sensor stream from the list of available feeds as shown in Figure 2-20.

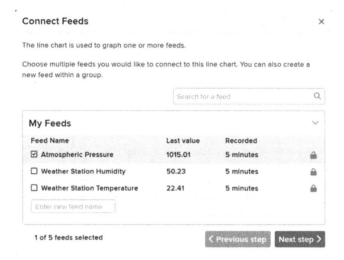

Figure 2-20. *Select a sensor stream*

In the next step, configure the sensor stream by assigning a title, labeling the axes, and adjusting the historical data window to one hour (Figure 2-21).

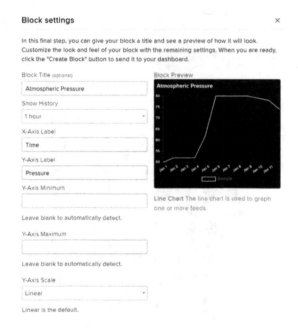

Figure 2-21. *Configure the sensor stream*

Repeat this process for all three sensor streams: Atmospheric Pressure, Temperature, and Humidity. Your dashboard should look like what is shown in Figure 2-22.

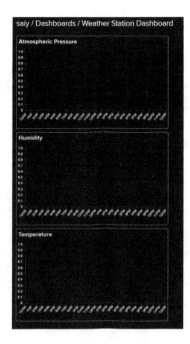

Figure 2-22. *Create Line Chart Blocks for all three sensor streams*

Now, it is time to rearrange the layout for better visualization. Under Dashboard Settings (the gear icon on the top right), click *Edit Layout*. Note that the dashboard is currently set to private (as shown in Figure 2-23). This ensures that only you can view the data.

Figure 2-23. *Edit Layout*

The dashboard was rearranged and saved to look like Figure 2-24.

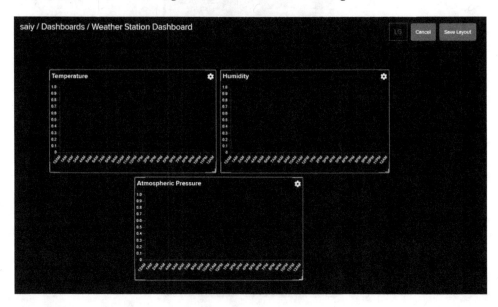

Figure 2-24. *Rearranged dashboard*

Now, you can access your dashboard from the *Dashboard* tab at the top of the page and review all sensor data on the dashboard (as shown in Figure 2-25). In this case, there are only three sensors. Imagine a scenario with a fleet of devices uploading three sensor streams each. How would you go about designing a dashboard for such an application?

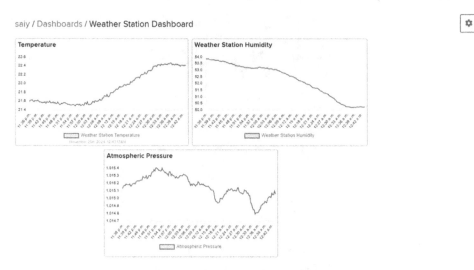

Figure 2-25. *Weather Station Dashboard*

In this example, we reviewed uploading temperature, humidity, and atmospheric data to the cloud. We challenge you to upload the windspeed data. How would you simulate windspeed?

Dashboard Considerations

While designing a dashboard, consider the view that is helpful to you or your customer. Your dashboard must highlight critical data points from the fleet and alerts received from sensors in the field. Regarding weather sensors, a change in wind speed could warrant an alert. The dashboard also needs to highlight units needing servicing or missing an alert.

When designing a dashboard highlighting units across the country, how would you create a dashboard that groups them? How do you service units that are installed so far apart?

Installation Considerations

Water ingress can damage electronics, and the design of electronics for outdoor use requires extraordinary precautions. This prototype must be waterproofed before it is installed outdoors.

IoT products meant for outdoor use need an enclosure rated for harsh environments, including the power source and the associated cabling required for your product. Testing labs can test your product for water ingress prevention, exposure to sunlight, etc. Some of these tests are critical to taking your product to the market.

If your product is going to be installed in a location away from a power source, how will you provide power to it? Any battery you choose must comply with the environment's temperature conditions and be rated for battery use. Can you use a solar panel?

Conclusion

In this chapter, we took a weather station example to review publishing sensor data to the cloud. We used Adafruit IO to upload sensor data and review it on a web dashboard. We also discussed using third-party libraries to retrieve the weather station data. The next chapter will discuss building visual aids for air quality.

CHAPTER 3

Visual Aid for Air Quality

In this chapter, we will learn how to build IoT products using public data sources or make decisions by combining local and public data sources. The intent is to construct a visual aid that helps vulnerable populations.

Project Description

This project is a visual aid for air quality. It can be used to understand current air quality conditions and obtain a forecast using local data sources. We will learn to integrate air quality sensors with the ESP32 and understand how to use libraries written by others to read sensor data. We will use the AirNow API to get a forecast of the local air quality. Ultimately, our visual aid should look like the one shown in Figure 3-1.

© Sai Yamanoor and Srihari Yamanoor 2025
S. Yamanoor and S. Yamanoor, *IoT Product Development Using ESP32 Microcontrollers*,
https://doi.org/10.1007/979-8-8688-1570-6_3

Figure 3-1. *Visual aid for air quality*

Product Case

Why do we need a visual aid? As cities around the world become more polluted, chronic health conditions like asthma are on the rise. Protecting a city's most vulnerable population is essential. A visual aid like this can help educate citizens about air quality in their neighborhoods.

Citizen scientists have a critical role to play in collecting air quality data at the neighborhood level. In this chapter, we wanted to demonstrate how IoT-enabled products can bring citizen science to the masses.

Figure 3-2 illustrates a product case where citizen scientists deploy wireless sensor nodes and upload air quality data from their vicinity. This enables the education of other citizens about the air quality in the general area. Without local data, a publicly available data source (like a government agency) could provide general guidance on air quality in a city. Products in the market follow this architecture.

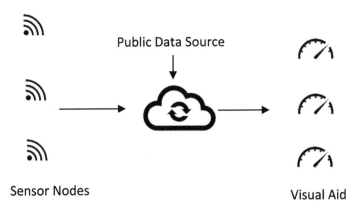

Figure 3-2. *Bringing citizen science to the masses with IoT*

This demonstrates the role IoT can play in bringing awareness about the environment. There are instances where local events have warned fellow citizens about a drop in the air quality index.

Components Used in This Project

Table 3-1 shows the components used in this chapter. We have designed this chapter to be "choose-your-own-adventure." Depending on your budget, you can choose to follow along and decide which features to implement in your project.

Table 3-1. *Components used in this chapter*

Item	Description	Price (in USD)	Link
1	Adafruit Metro ESP32-S3	24.95	https://www.adafruit.com/product/5500
2	2.8" TFT Touch Shield for Arduino with Capacitive Touch	44.95	https://www.adafruit.com/product/1947
3	SparkFun Indoor Air Quality – SCD41, SEN55	186.48	https://www.sparkfun.com/products/25200

We have chosen some expensive sensors for our recommended list of components. These are just examples to demonstrate interfacing air quality sensors and how to write or find open source drivers to integrate the sensor into your project. The SCD41 and SEN55 sensors are sold separately. They are available here: `https://www.sparkfun.com/products/22396` and `https://www.sparkfun.com/products/23715`, respectively. You are, of course, welcome to choose any sensor. You can also avoid integrating a sensor and retrieving data from a public data source, as we will demonstrate in this chapter. We will get started with installing the prerequisite libraries in the next section.

In the next section, we will discuss retrieving air quality data from a public cloud source.

Retrieving Data Using an API

We will retrieve data using an API (Application Programming Interface) to obtain local air quality data for your immediate surroundings. For our example, we will use the AirNow API (`https://www.airnow.gov`). This API is meant to provide air quality data using data sources from the United States, Canada, and Mexico. If you live in the European Union, we recommend checking out the Climate Data Store API: `https://eeadmz1-downloads-api-appservice.azurewebsites.net/swagger/index.html` or explore.openaq.org for the rest of the world. You can adapt the example in this section to the API available for your local air quality data.

An API, or Application Programming Interface, is a documented interface for communicating with a web or computer application. APIs enable users to create, read, update, or delete (commonly referred to as CRUD operations) data from a web server using the documented interface. If you are not familiar with the concept of APIs, we recommend checking out `https://www.ibm.com/topics/api`.

The AirNow API is a partnership between several agencies in the United States, such as the EPA, NOAA, etc. The AirNow API aggregates data from all the agencies and provides it to the public for free. They also collect air quality data from US embassies and consulates in other countries.

Obtaining an API Key

First, sign up for an API key from the AirNow website. You can sign up for an account for free at `https://docs.airnowapi.org/login`. Once you log in to your account, you can find the API key in the top right corner of the page under the Web Services tab (as shown with the red box in Figure 3-3). Save this information, as we will use it in our MicroPython code later.

Figure 3-3. *Location of the API Key (on the top right corner) on the AirNow API Web Services page*

Performing a Test Query

We will perform a test query using the query tool to retrieve the current observations. The API key is needed to retrieve data using the API. We can test the AirNow API using the query tool shown in Figure 3-5.

1. We will retrieve the current air quality observation for San Francisco, CA, using the query tool.

2. Selecting the query tool for *Current Observations By Zip Code* (shown in Figure 3-4) should launch a window, as shown in Figure 3-5. Let's set the zip code to *94103* and format to *application/json*.

Current Observations by Reporting Area

By Zip code
Get current AQI values and categories for a reporting area by Zip code.
Documentation   Query Tool

Figure 3-4. *Select Current Observations by Reporting Area*

Figure 3-5. *Set zip code and format*

3. When you click on Build, it should generate a URL (in the
   Generated URL text section), as shown in the snippet below:
   ```
   https://www.airnowapi.org/aq/observation/zipCode/
   current/?format=application/json&zipCode=95051&distanc
   e=15&API_KEY=ABCDEFG1234567890
   ```

4. When you run the generated URL using the *Run* button, we
   collect air quality data for a 5-mile radius of that zip code
   (as shown in Figure 3-6).

3 Output

```
[{"DateObserved":"2024-10-
23","HourObserved":17,"LocalTimeZone":"PST","ReportingArea":"San
Jose","StateCode":"CA","Latitude":37.33,"Longitude":-121.9,"ParameterName":"O3","AQI
":44,"Category":{"Number":1,"Name":"Good"}},{"DateObserved":"2024-10-
23","HourObserved":17,"LocalTimeZone":"PST","ReportingArea":"San
Jose","StateCode":"CA","Latitude":37.33,"Longitude":-121.9,"ParameterName":"PM2.5","
AQI":50,"Category":{"Number":1,"Name":"Good"}}]
```

Figure 3-6. *Air quality forecast for five days*

5. Let's take a closer look at the October 23, 2024 observation.
    According to the snippet shown below, the report indicates that
    the Air Quality Index for the Ozone gas parameter (O3) selected
    zip code is 44 and is categorized as *Good*. The PM2.5 parameter
    report indicates that the Air Quality Index is 50 and categorized
    as Good.

    ```
    [{"DateObserved":"2024-10-23","HourObserved":17,"LocalTimeZone":
    "PST","ReportingArea":"San Jose","StateCode":"CA","Latitude":
    37.33,"Longitude":-121.9,"ParameterName":"O3","AQI":44,"Category":
    {"Number":1,"Name":"Good"}},{"DateObserved":"2024-10-23",
    "HourObserved":17,"LocalTimeZone":"PST","ReportingArea":"San
    Jose","StateCode":"CA","Latitude":37.33,"Longitude":-121.9,
    "ParameterName":"PM2.5","AQI":50,"Category":{"Number":1,
    "Name":"Good"}}]
    ```

6. Let's build an understanding of the parameters and their corresponding
    observations. This is necessary for building our visual aid.

7. The current observation report contains data for two parameters,
    namely, Ozone (O3) and Particulate Matter 2.5 (PM2.5).

8. Particulate Matter 2.5 refers to particles in the air that are smaller
    than 2.5 micrometers in diameter. The presence of a large
    quantity of matter can cause conditions like asthma. The US
    Environmental Protection Agency (EPA) sets the standards for
    acceptable levels of particulate matter in the air.

9. Ozone gas is typically caused by air pollution and causes respiratory problems.

10. You will have noticed that the report contains the Air Quality Index, which is a number along with its corresponding category. The EPA calculates the Air Quality Index for Ozone based on an eight-hour average of the measured ozone levels. The Air Quality Index for Particulate Matter 2.5 is calculated using a 24-hour average of the measurements.

11. The Air Quality Index is color-coded and provided with a descriptor by the EPA. The various categories are shown in Figure 3-7.

AQI colors

The AQI is divided into color-coded categories and each category is identified by a simple informative descriptor. The descriptors are intended to convey information to the public about how air quality relates to public health. The table below defines the AQI categories.

AQI Numbers	AQI Category (Descriptor)	AQI Color	Hexadecimal Color Value	Category Number
0 - 50	Good	Green	(00e400)	1
51 - 100	Moderate	Yellow	(ffff00)	2
101 - 150	Unhealthy for Sensitive Groups	Orange	(ff7e00)	3
151 - 200	Unhealthy	Red	(ff0000)	4
201 - 300	Very Unhealthy	Purple	(8f3f97)	5
301 - 500	Hazardous	Maroon	(7e0023)	6

Figure 3-7. *Air Quality Index categorization (Source: Air Quality Now API Docs)*

12. For the report retrieved in this example, the Ozone AQI was 44 and the PM2.5 AQI was 50. According to the table, both parameters were qualified as good.

13. If the AQI levels are projected to exceed the moderate category, an *Action Day* alert is issued. This usually means that vulnerable populations need to take additional precautions such as staying indoors. The local authorities can also implement additional measures such as a temporary ban on burning wood logs.

Action Day alerts can be obtained using the Forecast Query Tool from the Web Services page shown in Figure 3-3. We recommend trying the forecast using the current observation example.

You can read more about the AirNow API at `https://docs.airnowapi.org/` aq101. Next, we will write code in MicroPython to retrieve the data we just discussed in this section to build our visual aid. Isn't it exciting to build a tool to help vulnerable populations? We hope that you are able to glean the role IoT can play in improving quality of life.

MicroPython Code for Retrieving AQI Data

As a first step, we will write some code in MicroPython to retrieve current observations using the AirNow API.

Creating secrets.py

In Thonny IDE, let's create a new file called secrets.py. We will store two variables, namely:

```
SSID = "MyWifi"
PASSWORD = "Password"
API_KEY = "ABCDEFG1234567890"
```

The SSID and PASSWORD refer to the credentials of your local Wi-Fi network. The API_ KEY refers to the key retrieved from your AirNow API account.

1. We will upload this code sample to the device. In the Thonny IDE, make sure that you view the file directory. This can be accomplished by going to View ➤ Files (as shown in Figure 3-8).

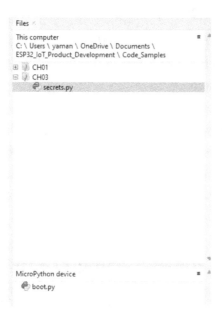

Figure 3-8. *Enable File Viewer in Thonny IDE*

2. At the top is the file directory of your computer. At the bottom is the file system of the Adafruit Metro ESP32-S3. We are going to upload this file to the MicroPython device.

3. Before we upload the file, we need to make sure that there is no active program running on the device. You can stop it by using the Stop button on the toolbar (Figure 3-9).

Figure 3-9. *Stop programs using the STOP button*

4. Right-click on *secrets.py* located in your local directory and select
    Upload to / (Figure 3-10).

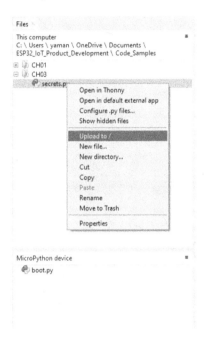

Figure 3-10. *Right-click and upload secrets.py*

5. This should upload secrets.py to our device and be visible in its
    file directory (as shown in Figure 3-11).

Figure 3-11. *secrets.py uploaded to Adafruit Metro ESP32-S3*

6. Now, we can use *secrets.py*, which contains the requisite credentials, in other code samples. This also helps avoid uploading our private credentials to a public code repository. You can just ignore *secrets.py* in your repository setup.

Next, we will review making use of *secrets.py* to retrieve current air quality observations using the AirNow API.

Using MicroPython to Retrieve Air Quality Data

In this section, we will write code using MicroPython to retrieve the current air quality report. The example discussed in this section is available for download along with this chapter as airnow_api_request_example.py.

In the example, we will use the URL generated earlier in this section to retrieve the report. But we will seek the user input for the zip code and distance parameters.

1. The first step in our code is to import the requisite modules. We need the network module to connect to the Wi-Fi network, time module for injecting delays in our code, the secrets module for network credentials, and finally the urequests module for placing a GET request to retrieve the air quality report.

```
import urequests
import network
import time
import secrets
```

2. Next, we declare the URL used to retrieve the current air quality data including the *?* separator used to supply the parameters for our request:

```
url = "https://www.airnowapi.org/aq/observation/zipCode/current/?"
```

3. Referring to the URL generated earlier, we need to supply the following parameters in our request, namely, zip code, distance radius, API key, and the data report format. In the snippet below, we declare the format and the API key in a dictionary called parameters. We will add the zip code and the distance radius parameters later in the code.

```
parameters = {
    "format" : "application/json",
    "API_KEY" : secrets.API_KEY
}
```

4. Next, we connect to our local Wi-Fi network using the network credentials stored in *secrets.py*. This part is identical to the example in Chapter 1 where we connect to the network and print the IP address of the device.

```
wlan = network.WLAN(network.STA_IF)
wlan.active(True)
wlan.connect(secrets.SSID, secrets.PASSWORD)
```

```
while not wlan.isconnected():
    print(".")
    time.sleep(1)

print(f"Success! Connected to {secrets.SSID}")
network_params = wlan.ifconfig()
print(f"IP address is {network_params[0]}")
```

5. Now, we capture the user input for zip code and the distance parameters using the input() function. We save the user input to the parameters dictionary using the zipCode and distance keys.

```
parameters["zipCode"] = input("Enter a valid zipcode: ")
parameters["distance"] = input("Enter distance radius: ")
```

6. Next, we iterate through the dictionary and add the parameters to the URL. The name of the parameters and their corresponding value are appended by inserting a = sign in between them. The parameters are separated using the & sign.

```
for key, value in parameters.items():
    url += key + "=" + value + "&"
```

7. We strip the last & using the rstrip() method from the URL as it is not needed and print the URL.

```
url = url.rstrip("&")
print(f"The URL is {url}")
```

8. Next, we use a try/except/else/finally block to retrieve the current air quality report.

```
try:
    response = urequests.get(url)
except Exception as error:
    print(error)
else:
    print(response.status_code)
    print(response.json())
finally:
    wlan.disconnect()
```

9. In the try block, we use the urequests module to make a GET
    request using the constructed URL.

    ```
    response = urequests.get(url)
    ```

10. In the except block, we handle any exception that might occur
    while making the GET request.

11. If the request succeeds, in the else block, we print the status code
    of the request and parse the response using the json() method.
    This is because we requested the report in JSON format.

12. The finally block is always executed irrespective of whether the
    GET request succeeds or an error occurs. Here, we disconnect from
    the Wi-Fi network.

Putting it all together, we have

```python
import urequests
import network
import time
import secrets

url = "https://www.airnowapi.org/aq/observation/zipCode/current/?"

parameters = {
    "format" : "application/json",
    "API_KEY" : secrets.API_KEY
}

wlan = network.WLAN(network.STA_IF)
wlan.active(True)
wlan.connect(secrets.SSID, secrets.PASSWORD)

while not wlan.isconnected():
    print(".")
    time.sleep(1)

print(f"Success! Connected to {secrets.SSID}")
network_params = wlan.ifconfig()
print(f"IP address is {network_params[0]}")
```

```
parameters["zipCode"] = input("Enter a valid zipcode: ")
parameters["distance"] = input("Enter distance radius: ")

for key, value in parameters.items():
    url += key + "=" + value + "&"

url = url.rstrip("&")
print(f"The URL is {url}")

try:
    response = urequests.get(url)
except Exception as error:
    print(error)
else:
    print(response.status_code)
    print(response.json())
finally:
    wlan.disconnect()
```

You can type in the above code sample and run it using the *Run Current Script* button from the Thonny editor (Figure 3-12).

Figure 3-12. *Run Current Script button*

1. When the script is launched, the ESP32 connects to the Wi-Fi network and is paused for user input (as shown in Figure 3-13).

```
Shell
>>> %Run -c $EDITOR_CONTENT

 MPY: soft reboot
 .
 .
 .
 .
 .
 .
 .
 .
 Success! Connected to
 IP address is 192.168.1.70
 Enter a valid zipcode:
```

Figure 3-13. *AirNow API script execution*

2. When we enter a valid zip code and distance radius, the script fetches the air quality data, parses it, and prints it along with the status code. The script also prints out the URL constructed using the user input. Figure 3-14 shows the script output where the status code is 200 and the parsed JSON shows that the air quality is *Good*.

```
MPY: soft reboot
Success! Connected to
IP address is 192.168.1.70
Enter a valid zipcode: 94103
Enter distance radius: 10
The URL is https://www.airnowapi.org/aq/observation/zipCode/current/?distance=10&API
KEY=                                  &format=application/json&zipCode=94103
200
[{'AQI': 33, 'HourObserved': 16, 'ReportingArea': 'San Francisco', 'DateObserved': '2
024-10-26', 'LocalTimeZone': 'PST', 'Latitude': 37.75, 'StateCode': 'CA', 'Category':
{'Number': 1, 'Name': 'Good'}, 'Longitude': -122.43, 'ParameterName': 'O3'}]
```

Figure 3-14. *AirNow API report*

Try executing the script with zip codes in your neighborhood. Are you aware of the air quality where you live or regularly visit? Try this script to learn more about it.

Did you know? The AirNow API provides air quality forecasts that warn citizens to protect vulnerable populations. They are known as *Action Days*. Consider modifying this script to obtain the air quality forecast. You can learn more about the forecast API from the AirNow API documentation. The forecast example is available for download along with this chapter as *airnow_api_forecast_example.py*.

Data Use Guidelines

The AirNow API is meant for end users to query air quality data and become more aware of their surroundings. The API permits a user to make up to 500 requests in an hour. What if you build a product to be deployed across the United States?

Consider a scenario where you will deploy hundreds or thousands of units across North America. In this case, the AirNow API provides a file service called File Products. It enables querying for a file that contains the air quality observations for all zip codes. You can query for the file once an hour and update your database. You need to build a database to parse through the file and populate the data. The devices you deploy to various zip codes will query this database to retrieve the air quality data for the corresponding zip code. An architecture of this product is illustrated in Figure 3-15.

If you build a product using the AirNow API, you must credit the API. This could be on your product's website or in the visual aid. You can read more about the data usage guidelines at `https://docs.airnowapi.org/docs/DataUseGuidelines.pdf`.

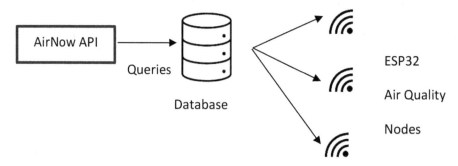

Figure 3-15. *AirQuality Node product built using the AirNow API*

In this section, we learned how to retrieve data from public sources to build a product. Next, we will learn how to interface air quality sensors with the ESP32.

Interfacing Air Quality Sensors to the ESP32

In this section, we will discuss interfacing air quality sensors to the Adafruit Metro ESP32-S3. As mentioned earlier, we will use the SparkFun Indoor Air Quality Combo Sensor (shown in Figure 3-16). The sensor kit consists of the SCD41 and SEN55 sensors from Sensirion (`https://sensirion.com/`). The SEN55 measures environmental parameters, such as particulate matter (PM1.0, 2.5, 4, and 10), volatile organic compounds, and nitrogen oxides (NO_x). The SCD41 is a carbon dioxide sensor capable of measuring concentrations in the range of 400–1000 ppm. It has an accuracy of ±50 ppm.

Figure 3-16. *SparkFun Air Quality Combo Sensor (Image source: SparkFun License: CC BY 2.0)*

Apart from demonstrating sensor integration of sensors to the ESP32, we will also show how to write drivers for any sensor you choose for your product. Let's get started.

Sensor Selection

The first step in integrating a sensor into a product is determining how to integrate and use the sensor. Sensors come with various outputs, such as analog voltage, 4–20 mA, serial output, etc. Besides considering whether the sensor can be integrated with your microcontroller, you must also consider whether it suits your application. For example, analog signals can be very noisy and require a lot of signal conditioning. If your sensor is installed far away from the microcontroller, a sensor with a 4–20 mA output is appropriate.

In this project, we chose sensors with an I²C output. The sensor comes with built-in signal conditioning elements, which helps us focus on building our prototype rather than the sensor signal conditioning.

A sensor with an I²C output has limitations. Due to the bus capacitance, I²C interfaces are unsuitable for long-distance transmissions. Differential I²C transceivers can help mitigate this problem, but this is not an issue for this project.

I²C Communication Interface

I²C (Inter-Integrated Circuit) interface is a type of synchronous serial communication where multiple sensors can communicate with the microcontroller using the communication bus. An I²C bus consists of two lines: the serial data clock (SCL) and the serial data line (SDA). The microcontroller is the host and drives the clock. The sensors connected to an I²C bus have a unique address. The host drives communication to all sensors or any peripheral connected to the bus. Figure 3-17 illustrates the sensors and their addresses (in hex format) connected to the Adafruit Metro ESP32-S3's I²C bus, including the sensor kit in this section. The SCL and SDA pins of the sensor are connected to that of the ESP32-S3 MCU.

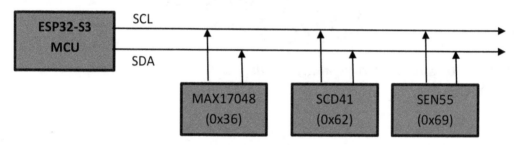

Figure 3-17. *Sensors connected to the ESP32-S3's I²C bus*

Figure 3-17 shows that each sensor connected to the ESP32-S3 has a unique address. This enables the host to communicate with the sensor using that address. Suppose we need the microcontroller to talk to two sensors with the same address. In that case, we have two options:

1. Use an I²C multiplexer to connect the sensor to the individual channels and switch channels to communicate with the sensors. Here is an example of an 8-channel I²C multiplexer: https://www.sparkfun.com/products/16784

2. Use an I²C address translator where we change the device's address on the fly. Here is an example of an I²C address translator: https://www.adafruit.com/product/5914

For a deep dive into I²C communication, we recommend checking out the following article: https://learn.sparkfun.com/tutorials/i2c/all.

Qwiic Connect System

SparkFun introduced a prototyping ecosystem for I²C devices. Qwiic-compatible devices have a four-pin connector designed to carry the following signals: SCL, SDA, 3.3V, and Ground. Qwiic-compatible prototyping tools can be daisy-chained to connect multiple I²C devices. Figure 3-18 shows the Qwiic connector on the Adafruit Metro ESP32-S3 and the SparkFun Indoor Air Quality Combo Sensor.

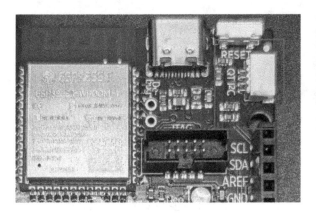

Figure 3-18. *Location of the Qwiic connector. License for the image on the right: CC-by-SA 2.0*

There are Qwiic-compatible boards from SparkFun, Adafruit, and other manufacturers. These boards include OLED displays, sensors, motor controllers, etc. Qwiic-compatible boards usually have two connectors. This enables us to daisy-chain boards together and thus prove a product's concept before we move on to the design stage. The boards are connected using a four-color Qwiic cable (shown in Figure 3-19). These cables come in different lengths and are crimped with mating connectors for the Qwiic interface. The cables are color-coded, and the colors are mapped to each signal as follows:

- Red → 3.3V

- Black → Ground

- Blue → SDA

- Yellow → SCL

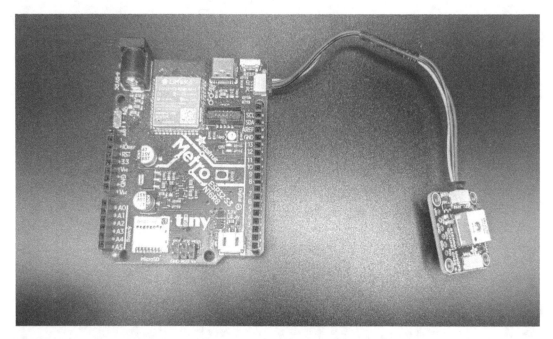

Figure 3-19. *A sensor connected to the Adafruit Metro ESP32-S3 using a four-color Qwiic cable*

Qwiic boards from SparkFun support only 3.3V signals. However, the Qwiic-compatible breakout boards from Adafruit, called Stemma, support 5V signals. You must know the nomenclature and be careful when selecting a Qwiic-compatible board for your project.

Next, we will write some code to scan for sensors using the Adafruit Metro ESP32-S3 board.

Performing an I²C Bus Scan

Let's ensure our sensors are operational with some simple MicroPython code. The SparkFun Indoor Air Quality Combo Sensor is interfaced with the development board using a Qwiic cable (Figure 3-20).

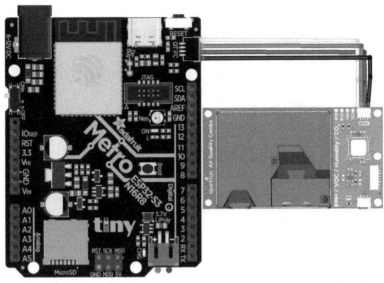

Figure 3-20. *Adafruit Metro ESP32-S3 interfaced to the Sparkfun Air Quality Combo*

Let's get started! The example discussed in this section is available for download along with this chapter as *ch03_i2c_bus_scan.py*.

1. The first step is to import the SoftI2C class from the machine module. SoftI2C refers to software-based I²C communication. Instead of using the hardware I²C interface, we use a software interface that emulates it because it has some timing issues.

   ```
   from machine import SoftI2C
   ```

2. We create an instance of the SoftI2C class and call it i2c. We set the SCL pin to GPIO 48, SDA to GPIO 47, and the I²C clock frequency to 400 kHz. Referring to Figure 1-11 in the first chapter. From the pinout diagram, we know that the SCL and SDA pins of the Qwiic connector are set to GPIO 48 and 47, respectively.

   ```
   i2c = SoftI2C(scl=48, sda=47, freq=400000)
   ```

3. Now, we can scan devices on the I²C bus by calling the scan() method. The method returns a list of addresses in decimal format. We convert it to a hexadecimal number using list comprehension. We also print it to the terminal by unpacking the list.

```
results = [hex(address) for address in i2c.scan()]
print("The devices on the I2C bus are:", *results)
```

4. Putting it all together, we have

```
from machine import SoftI2C

i2c = SoftI2C(scl=48, sda=47, freq=400000)
print("The devices on the I2C bus are:", i2c.scan())
```

When we run the above code sample using the *Run Current Script* button from the Thonny editor, we get the output shown in Figure 3-21. If your development board is running another program, stop it using the Stop button before running this script.

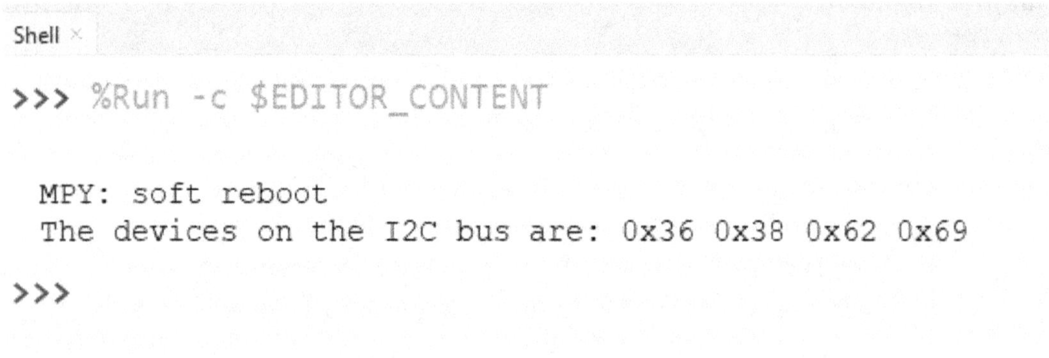

```
Shell ×

>>> %Run -c $EDITOR_CONTENT


MPY: soft reboot
The devices on the I2C bus are: 0x36 0x38 0x62 0x69

>>>
```

Figure 3-21. *I²C bus scan output*

The scan script's result shows that four devices were detected on the I²C bus. Let's try to identify them using the datasheets of the components we know are connected to the bus. The links to the datasheets are available at the end of this chapter.

1. SCD41: The device address is 0x62.

2. SEN55: The device address is 0x69.

3. Referring to the features of the Adafruit Metro ESP32-S3, we know that it has a MAX17048 Battery Monitor. Its address is 0x36.

4. For the visual aid, a TFT LCD Display is stacked on top of the Metro. The display has a capacitive touchscreen controller whose address is 0x38.

Now that we have identified all the devices on the bus, we will review the drivers for SCD41 and SEN55.

Drivers for SCD41 and SEN55

A software driver is code that follows a documented communication protocol. The driver handles all communication through the I²C interfaces. It parses the raw data and returns actionable sensor data. Typically, drivers are written using the commands presented in the sensor documentation or the application note provided by the manufacturer.

Because of the large user base in the MicroPython community, some contributors have probably written the drivers needed for our sensors. You could use those drivers if you build a proof-of-concept prototype or if the community actively maintains them. The drivers might come with a license that is incompatible with creating a commercial product.

In this section, we will modify the Python drivers provided by the manufacturer, Sensirion, to make them suitable for MicroPython. The drivers come with a BSD-3 license, which permits redistribution and modification provided the original license is retained. You can read more about the BSD-3 license at `https://opensource.org/license/bsd-3-clause`. Sensirion's BSD-3 license enables use in commercial products. Let's get started with modifying the drivers. The MicroPython drivers discussed in this section are available for download along with this chapter under the folder *sensirion-drivers*.

The Python I²C driver is a common component of both drivers. It enables communication between the microcontroller and the sensor. The driver can be adapted for any platform. Sensirion provides an example of adapting the drivers for Linux-based devices like the Raspberry Pi. We will demonstrate how to modify the driver for MicroPython.

MicroPython I²C Driver for SCD41 and SEN55

The driver discussed in this section is suitable for both the SCD41 and SEN55 sensors. The Python I²C driver is available from `https://github.com/Sensirion/python-i2c-driver`. We forked the repository to modify the driver for the MicroPython platform, and our repository is available here: `https://github.com/sai-ydev/micropython-sensirion-i2c-driver`. The driver is also available under the *sensirion_i2c_driver* folder along with this chapter. Let's get started by installing the prerequisites.

Installing Prerequisite Libraries

In this section, we will install the libraries needed for the examples discussed in this chapter. The first prerequisite is the `logging` library. We must install the `logging` library using the MicroPython package manager, *mip*. mip comes pre-installed with your MicroPython binary if you are running version 1.20 or later. If you are connected to the network on your development board, the `logging` module can be installed as follows:

```
>>> import mip
>>> mip.install("logging")
```

We made your life easier by putting together a script that installs the `logging` library alongside the libraries we will discuss in the next section for you after connecting to the network. This script is available for download along with this chapter as *ch03_logging_mip_install.py*.

```
import network
import secrets
import mip
import time

wlan = network.WLAN(network.STA_IF)
wlan.active(True)
wlan.connect(secrets.SSID, secrets.PASSWORD)

while not wlan.isconnected():
    print(".")
    time.sleep(1)
```

```
print(f"Success! Connected to {secrets.SSID}")
network_params = wlan.ifconfig()
print(f"IP address is {network_params[0]}")

mip.install("logging")
mip.install("github:peterhinch/micropython-nano-gui")
mip.install("github:peterhinch/micropython-nano-gui/drivers/ili93xx")
```

Running this script from the Thonny IDE should install the `logging`, `micropython-nano-gui`, and `ili93xx` display drivers. The mip.install() command shows the installation progress as shown in Figure 3-22.

```
Success! Connected to
IP address is 192.168.230.119
Installing logging (latest) from https://micropython.org/pi/v2 to /lib
Copying: /lib/logging.mpy
Done
Installing github:peterhinch/micropython-nano-gui/package.json to /lib
Copying: /lib/gui/core/__init__.py
Copying: /lib/gui/core/colors.py
Copying: /lib/gui/core/fplot.py
Copying: /lib/gui/core/nanogui.py
Copying: /lib/gui/core/writer.py
Copying: /lib/gui/fonts/arial_50.py
Copying: /lib/gui/fonts/arial10.py
Copying: /lib/gui/fonts/arial35.py
Copying: /lib/gui/fonts/courier20.py
Copying: /lib/gui/fonts/font6.py
Copying: /lib/gui/fonts/font10.py
Copying: /lib/gui/fonts/freesans20.py
Copying: /lib/gui/widgets/__init__.py
Copying: /lib/gui/widgets/dial.py
Copying: /lib/gui/widgets/label.py
Copying: /lib/gui/widgets/led.py
Copying: /lib/gui/widgets/meter.py
Copying: /lib/gui/widgets/scale.py
Copying: /lib/gui/widgets/textbox.py
Copying: /lib/gui/widgets/__init__.py
Copying: /lib/gui/demos/aclock_large.py
Copying: /lib/gui/demos/aclock.py
Copying: /lib/gui/demos/aclock_ttgo.py
Copying: /lib/gui/demos/alevel.py
Copying: /lib/gui/demos/asnano.py
Copying: /lib/gui/demos/asnano_sync.py
Copying: /lib/gui/demos/clock_batt.py
Copying: /lib/gui/demos/clocktest.py
Copying: /lib/gui/demos/color15.py
Copying: /lib/gui/demos/color96.py
Copying: /lib/gui/demos/epd29_async.py
Copying: /lib/gui/demos/epd29_lowpower.py
Copying: /lib/gui/demos/epd29_sync.py
Copying: /lib/gui/demos/epd_async.py
Copying: /lib/gui/demos/fpt.py
Copying: /lib/gui/demos/mono_test.py
Copying: /lib/gui/demos/scale.py
Copying: /lib/gui/demos/sharptest.py
Copying: /lib/gui/demos/tbox.py
Done
Installing github:peterhinch/micropython-nano-gui/drivers/ili93xx/package.json to /lib
Copying: /lib/drivers/ili93xx/ili9341.py
Copying: /lib/drivers/ili93xx/ili9341_8bit.py
Copying: /lib/drivers/boolpalette.py
Done
```

Figure 3-22. *mip.install() command output*

Now that we have installed the prerequisite library, let's discuss the modifications to make it compatible with MicroPython.

Modifying I²C Drivers for Sensirion Sensors

1. The future statements located at the top of all files inside the *sensirion-i2c-driver* folder are commented out. This is because future statements are not supported in MicroPython.

   ```
   #from __future__ import absolute_import, division, print_function
   ```

2. The file *transceiver_v1.py* was copied and renamed as *micropython_transceiver.py*. This file contains the instructions needed to implement a MicroPython I²C interface for all sensors from Sensirion.

3. The I2cTransceiverV1 class was renamed to MicroPythonI2cTransceiver.

4. The __init__ method was modified to pass an instance of the I²C interface.

   ```
   def __init__(self, i2c_interface):
           super(MicroPythonI2cTransceiver, self).__init__()
           self._device = i2c_interface
   ```

5. The driver attribute methods description and channel_count were modified. The description method returns a string, while the channel_count returns None since it is a single-channel I²C interface. You can read about the methods in the doc strings corresponding to the methods in the file.

6. The transceive method was implemented to transmit and receive data from any I²C device. The line raise NotImplementedError() was removed. The transceive method accepts the following parameters: tx_data, rx_length, read_delay, and timeout.

7. If there is valid data to transmit, i.e., the parameter tx_data is not None, the data is written to the I²C device using the writeto method of MicroPython's I²C class.

   ```
   if tx_data is not None:
       try:
           self._device.writeto(slave_address, bytes(tx_data))
   ```

```
    except OSError:
        status = self.STATUS_UNSPECIFIED_ERROR
        log.exception("I2C TX Failure")
```

8. If there is a delay needed between a write and read transaction, the parameter read_delay is greater than 0. Then, a delay is introduced by calling the sleep method from the time module and the read_delay parameter is passed as the argument.

```
if read_delay:
            time.sleep(read_delay)
```

9. If rx_length is greater than 0, and the I²C write transaction was successful, data is read from the I²C device using the read_ from method.

```
if rx_length and status == self.STATUS_OK:
    try:
        rx_data = self._device.readfrom(slave_address, rx_length)
    except OSError:
        status = self.STATUS_UNSPECIFIED_ERROR
        log.exception("I2C RX Failure")
```

10. Finally the parameters status, error (error_code), and rx_data (received data) are returned as a tuple.

11. In __init__.py, the following line was removed:

```
from .linux_i2c_transceiver import LinuxI2cTransceiver #
noqa: F401
```

12. Then, the following line was added:

```
from .micropython_transceiver import MicroPythonI2cTransceiver
```

As mentioned earlier, the modified driver is available for download along with this chapter. Now that we have the I²C driver, we will discuss the modifications to the SEN55 sensor driver.

SEN55 MicroPython Driver

The SEN55 driver is an API that makes use of the I²C driver discussed in the previous section to communicate with the sensor. The Sensirion SEN55 sensor driver is available under a BSD-3 license here: `https://github.com/Sensirion/python-i2c-sen5x`. The driver was modified for MicroPython and made available here: `https://github.com/sai-ydev/micropython-i2c-sen5x`. The modified driver is also available for download along with this chapter under the `sensirion_i2c_sen5x`.

The modifications made to the driver are as follows:

1. The future statement located at the top of `generated.py` inside the `sensirion_i2c_sen5x` folder is commented out. This is because future statements are not supported in MicroPython.

   ```
   #from __future__ import absolute_import, division, print_function
   ```

2. The line number 223 was modified as follows:

   ```
   data_ready = bool(checked_data[1])
   ```

3. The line number 1122 was modified as follows:

   ```
   firmware_debug = bool(checked_data[2])
   ```

The modifications to the code were based on trial and error. We tried making use of the driver and made modifications according to the error generated.

SEN55 Interface Example

Now that we have the drivers ready, let's take the SEN55 for a spin. The SparkFun Air Quality Combo kit is interfaced to the Adafruit Metro ESP32-S3 as shown in Figure 3-20. The example discussed in this section is based on the documentation from `https://sensirion.github.io/python-i2c-sen5x/quickstart.html#linux-i2c-bus-example`. The example discussed in this section is available for download along with this chapter as *ch03_sen55_example.py*.

Let's discuss the example:

1. The first step is the imports needed for the example.
   This includes the I2C class from the machine library,
   MicroPythonI2cTransceiver and I2cConnection from the
   sensirion_i2c_driver library, and the Sen5xI2cDevice from
   sensirion_i2c_sen5x library.

```
import time
from machine import I2C
from sensirion_i2c_driver import I2cConnection,
MicroPythonI2cTransceiver
from sensirion_i2c_sen5x import Sen5xI2cDevice
```

2. Then, we initialize the I²C interface with the SCL pin as 48 and SDA
   pin as 47 and set the frequency of the interface to 400 kHz.

```
i2c = I2C(scl=48, sda=47, freq=400000)
```

3. We pass the i2c object and create an instance of the
   MicroPythonI2cTransceiver class. Then, we create an instance
   of the Sen5xI2cDevice class for communications with the
   SEN55 sensor.

```
i2c = I2C(scl=48, sda=47, freq=400000)
i2c_transceiver = MicroPythonI2cTransceiver(i2c)
device = Sen5xI2cDevice(I2cConnection(i2c_transceiver))
```

4. Now, we print some device information including version,
   product name, and its serial number. This is performed by
   calling methods of the Sen5xI2cDevice class which in turn sends
   commands to the SEN55 sensor using the i2c_transceiver object
   via the I²C interface.

```
print("Version: {}".format(device.get_version()))
print("Product Name: {}".format(device.get_product_name()))
print("Serial Number: {}".format(device.get_serial_number()))
```

5. We perform a reset of the SEN55 sensor and start the measurements.

```
device.device_reset()
device.start_measurement()
```

6. We enter a for loop that runs 1000 times where we check whether a new data sample is ready from the SEN55 sensor. We retrieve the measured values and print them. This includes PM1.0, PM2.5, PM4.0, and PM10.0 concentrations. We also print the ambient temperature and humidity, VOC, and NOx index values.

```
for _ in range(1000):
    # Wait until next result is available
    print("Waiting for new data...")
    while device.read_data_ready() is False:
        time.sleep(0.1)

    # Read measured values -> clears the "data ready" flag
    values = device.read_measured_values()
    print(values)

    # Access a specific value separately (see Sen5xMeasuredValues)
    mass_concentration = values.mass_concentration_2p5.physical
    ambient_temperature = values.ambient_temperature.
    degrees_celsius

    # Read device status
    status = device.read_device_status()
    print("Device Status: {}\n".format(status))
```

7. The method read_measured_values prints out all the data. It is also possible to retrieve the individual concentrations as shown in the snippet below. You can read more about the methods available to retrieve the individual concentrations here: https://sensirion.github.io/python-i2c-sen5x/api.html#sen5xmeasuredvalues

```
mass_concentration = values.mass_concentration_2p5.physical
ambient_temperature = values.ambient_temperature.degrees_celsius
```

8. We can read the device status using the read_device_
   status method.

```
status = device.read_device_status()
print("Device Status: {}\n".format(status))
```

9. Upon exiting the for loop, we stop the measurement using the
   stop_measurement method, which sends a command to the
   SEN55 sensor.

```
device.stop_measurement()
print("Measurement stopped.")
```

Putting it all together, we have

```
import time
from machine import I2C
from sensirion_i2c_driver import I2cConnection, MicroPythonI2cTransceiver
from sensirion_i2c_sen5x import Sen5xI2cDevice

i2c = I2C(scl=48, sda=47, freq=400000)
i2c_transceiver = MicroPythonI2cTransceiver(i2c)
device = Sen5xI2cDevice(I2cConnection(i2c_transceiver))

# Print some device information
print("Version: {}".format(device.get_version()))
print("Product Name: {}".format(device.get_product_name()))
print("Serial Number: {}".format(device.get_serial_number()))

# Perform a device reset (reboot firmware)
device.device_reset()

# Start measurement
device.start_measurement()
for _ in range(1000):
    # Wait until next result is available
    print("Waiting for new data...")
    while device.read_data_ready() is False:
        time.sleep(0.1)
```

```
    # Read measured values -> clears the "data ready" flag
    values = device.read_measured_values()
    print(values)

    # Access a specific value separately (see Sen5xMeasuredValues)
    mass_concentration = values.mass_concentration_2p5.physical
    ambient_temperature = values.ambient_temperature.degrees_celsius

    # Read device status
    status = device.read_device_status()
    print("Device Status: {}\n".format(status))

# Stop measurement
device.stop_measurement()
print("Measurement stopped.")
```

When we run the script using the *Run Current Script* button from Thonny IDE, we get the following output over a loop over 1000 times:

```
Waiting for new data...
Mass Concentration PM1.0:     5.0 µg/m^3
Mass Concentration PM2.5:     5.2 µg/m^3
Mass Concentration PM4.0:     5.2 µg/m^3
Mass Concentration PM10.0:    5.2 µg/m^3
Ambient Humidity:             40.31 %RH
Ambient Temperature:          22.14 °C
VOC Index:                    101.0
NOx Index:                    1.0
Device Status: 0x00000000 [OK]

Measurement stopped.
```

Now that we have tested the SEN55 sensor, we will next review the drivers for the SCD41 sensor.

SCD41 MicroPython Driver

The SCD41 driver is an API that makes use of the I²C driver discussed earlier to communicate with the sensor. The Sensirion SCD41 sensor driver is available under a BSD-3 license here: https://github.com/Sensirion/python-i2c-scd. The driver was modified for MicroPython and made available here: https://github.com/sai-ydev/MicroPython-i2c-scd. The modified driver is also available for download along with this chapter under the sensirion_i2c_scd.

The modifications include the following:

1. The future statements located at the top of all files inside the *sensirion-i2c-scd* folder are commented out. This is because future statements are not supported in MicroPython.

   ```
   #from __future__ import absolute_import, division, print_function
   ```

2. In data_types.py, we commented out IntEnum class import as it is not supported, and we added the following line at the top:

   ```
   #from enum import IntEnum
   IntEnum = object
   ```

The modifications to the code were based on trial and error. We tried making use of the driver and made modifications according to the error generated. Next, we will take the scd driver for a spin to read CO_2 concentrations.

SCD41 Interface Example

The SCD41 interface example discussed in this section is available for download along with this chapter as ch03_scd41_example.py. The example is based on the Linux I²C example available from the Sensirion I²C SCD documentation: https://sensirion.github.io/python-i2c-scd/quickstart.html#execute-measurements-using-internal-linux-i2c-driver.

1. The first step is the imports needed for the example. This includes the I2C class from the machine library, MicroPythonI2cTransceiver and I2cConnection from the sensirion_i2c_driver library, and the Scd4xI2cDevice from the sensirion_i2c_scd library.

```
import time
from machine import I2C
from sensirion_i2c_driver import MicroPythonI2cTransceiver,
I2cConnection
from sensirion_i2c_scd import Scd4xI2cDevice
```

2. Then, we initialize the I²C interface with the SCL pin as 48 and SDA
    pin as 47 and set the frequency of the interface to 400 kHz.

```
i2c = I2C(scl=48, sda=47, freq=400000)
```

3. We pass the i2c object and create an instance of the
    MicroPythonI2cTransceiver class. Then, we create an instance
    of the Scd4xI2cDevice class for communications with the
    SCD41 sensor.

```
i2c = I2C(scl=48, sda=47, freq=400000)
i2c_transceiver = MicroPythonI2cTransceiver(i2c)
scd4x = Scd4xI2cDevice(I2cConnection(i2c_transceiver))
```

4. To read the sensor's serial number, we need to stop the periodic
    measurements by calling the stop_periodic_measurement
    method. We read the serial number using the read_serial_
    number method. Then, we start the periodic measurement using
    the start_periodic_measurement method.

```
scd4x.stop_periodic_measurement()
print("scd4x Serial Number: {}".format(scd4x.read_serial_
number()))
scd4x.start_periodic_measurement()
```

5. We enter a for loop and print the CO_2 concentration alongside the
    temperature and humidity data for 100 times.

```
for _ in range(100):
    time.sleep(5)
    co2, temperature, humidity = scd4x.read_measurement()
    # use default formatting for printing output:
    print("{}, {}, {}".format(co2, temperature, humidity))
```

6.   Finally, we stop the periodic measurement:

```
scd4x.stop_periodic_measurement()
print("Measurement stopped.")
```

Putting it all together, we have

```
import time
from machine import I2C
from sensirion_i2c_driver import MicroPythonI2cTransceiver, I2cConnection
from sensirion_i2c_scd import Scd4xI2cDevice

i2c = I2C(scl=48, sda=47, freq=400000)
i2c_transceiver = MicroPythonI2cTransceiver(i2c)
scd4x = Scd4xI2cDevice(I2cConnection(i2c_transceiver))

# Make sure measurement is stopped, else we can't read serial number or
# start a new measurement
scd4x.stop_periodic_measurement()

print("scd4x Serial Number: {}".format(scd4x.read_serial_number()))

scd4x.start_periodic_measurement()

# Measure every 5 seconds for 5 minute
for _ in range(100):
    time.sleep(5)
    co2, temperature, humidity = scd4x.read_measurement()
    # use default formatting for printing output:
    print("{}, {}, {}".format(co2, temperature, humidity))

scd4x.stop_periodic_measurement()
print("Measurement stopped.")
```

When we run the script using the *Run Current Script* button from the Thonny IDE, the following output is observed:

```
1071 ppm, 20.9 °C, 47.6 %RH
1069 ppm, 20.9 °C, 47.6 %RH
1066 ppm, 20.9 °C, 47.6 %RH
1062 ppm, 20.9 °C, 47.5 %RH
```

```
1061 ppm, 20.9 °C, 47.5 %RH
1060 ppm, 20.9 °C, 47.5 %RH
1058 ppm, 20.9 °C, 47.5 %RH
1056 ppm, 20.9 °C, 47.5 %RH
1054 ppm, 20.9 °C, 47.5 %RH
Measurement stopped.
```

Now that we have tested the sensors, we are going to focus on building our visual aid.

Building the Visual Aid

In this section, we are going to discuss building the visual aid using the sensors we interfaced with earlier. The visual aid is going to be a display that provides live updates of three parameters as they are measured. The example discussed in this chapter is available for download along with this chapter as *ch03_visual_aid.py*. The visual aid discussed in this section is a combination of examples discussed earlier.

The *micropython-nano-gui* library is required for this section. We showed how to install this library in the previous section. This library includes the drivers needed for the most common display drivers. The *Adafruit 2.8″ TFT Shield v2* makes use of the ILI9341 display driver.

Display Setup

The display driver is imported and initialized in a separate file called *color_setup.py* (available for download along with this chapter).

1. The first step is importing the Pin class and SPI class from the machine module.

    ```
    from machine import Pin, SPI
    ```

2. Next, we import the garbage collector module:

    ```
    import gc
    ```

3. We import the ILI9341 driver class for initializing and driving the display.

    ```
    from drivers.ili93xx.ili9341 import ILI9341 as SSD
    ```

4. We initialize the pins needed for the driver. This includes the Data
   Command/Select pin (pdc – GPIO Pin 9), the Reset pin (prst –
   GPIO Pin 8), and the Chip Select pin (pcs – GPIO Pin 10).

```
pdc = Pin(9, Pin.OUT, value=0)
prst = Pin(8, Pin.OUT, value=1)
pcs = Pin(10, Pin.OUT, value=1)
```

5. According to the display documentation from Adafruit, the display
   connects to the Metro board through the *ICSP port*. Refer to the
   ICSP pinout from Chapter 1. The pinout is as follows:
   SCK ➤ GPIO 39
   MOSI ➤ GPIO42
   MISO ➤ GPIO21

6. Now, we initialize the SPI port 1 as shown below where we set the
   clock frequency to 10 MHz:

```
spi = SPI(1, sck=Pin(39), mosi=Pin(42), miso=Pin(21),
baudrate=10_000_000)
```

7. Finally, we initialize the display with SPI interface object and the
   pins we defined for DC, RST, and CS. We also perform a garbage
   collection (clean-up of resources) before we set up the display.

```
gc.collect()
ssd = SSD(spi, cs=pcs, dc=pdc, rst=prst)
```

Putting it all together, we have

```
from machine import Pin, SPI
import gc
from drivers.ili93xx.ili9341 import ILI9341 as SSD

pdc = Pin(9, Pin.OUT, value=0)
prst = Pin(8, Pin.OUT, value=1)
pcs = Pin(10, Pin.OUT, value=1)
spi = SPI(1, sck=Pin(39), mosi=Pin(42), miso=Pin(21), baudrate=10_000_000)

gc.collect()
ssd = SSD(spi, cs=pcs, dc=pdc, rst=prst)
```

Save this code as color_setup.py and upload it to the Adafruit Metro ESP32-S3. Follow the same process as uploading secrets.py to the device.

Visual Aid Code

1. The first step is the library imports needed for this example. Two types of imports are needed. The first is the drivers and the GUI elements needed to build our visual aid. This also includes *color_setup.py* for initializing the display.

```
import utime # for delays
# display related imports
from color_setup import ssd  # Create a display instance
from gui.core.nanogui import refresh
from gui.widgets.meter import Meter
from gui.widgets.label import Label
import gui.fonts.arial10 as arial10
from gui.core.writer import Writer, CWriter
from gui.core.colors import *
```

2. The second set of imports is the libraries needed for the air quality sensors.

```
# sensor related imports
from machine import I2C
from sensirion_i2c_driver import MicroPythonI2cTransceiver,
I2cConnection
from sensirion_i2c_scd import Scd4xI2cDevice
from sensirion_i2c_sen5x import Sen5xI2cDevice
```

3. We initialize the I²C interface followed by the sensor communication objects.

```
i2c = I2C(scl=48, sda=47, freq=400000)
i2c_transceiver = MicroPythonI2cTransceiver(i2c)
scd4x = Scd4xI2cDevice(I2cConnection(i2c_transceiver))
sen5x = Sen5xI2cDevice(I2cConnection(i2c_transceiver))
```

4. This is followed by reading the serial number of the SCD41 and
    SEN55 sensors.

```
scd4x.stop_periodic_measurement()
print("scd4x Serial Number: {}".format(scd4x.read_serial_number()))
scd4x.start_periodic_measurement()

print("Version: {}".format(sen5x.get_version()))
print("Product Name: {}".format(sen5x.get_product_name()))
print("Serial Number: {}".format(sen5x.get_serial_number()))

sen5x.device_reset()
sen5x.start_measurement()
```

5. We clear the display and initialize the GUI writer object.

```
refresh(ssd, True)
CWriter.set_textpos(ssd, 0, 0)
wri = CWriter(ssd, arial10, GREEN, BLACK, verbose=False)
wri.set_clip(True, True, False)
```

6. We are going to be monitoring the CO_2 concentration, VOC index,
    and PM2.5 concentrations using this visual aid. We are going to
    create three objects belonging to the Meter class that display the
    data as a percentage of the total range of the sensor.

```
co2_meter = Meter(wri, 5, 2, height = 80, divisions = 40,
ptcolor=YELLOW,
            label='', style=Meter.BAR, legends=('400', '2300',
            '5000'))

voc_meter = Meter(wri, 5, 102, height = 80, divisions = 40,
ptcolor=YELLOW,
            label='', style=Meter.BAR, legends=('0',
            '250', '500'))

p25_meter = Meter(wri, 5, 202, height = 80, divisions = 40,
ptcolor=YELLOW,
            label='', style=Meter.BAR, legends=('0', '50.0',
            '100.0'))
```

7. Then, we create three objects of the Label class that are same as the Meter class objects.

```
co2_data_width = wri.stringlen('0000 ppm')
co2_label = Label(wri, 100, 0, 'CO2:')
co2_value_label = Label(wri, 100, 25, co2_data_width,
bdcolor=YELLOW)

voc_index_width = wri.stringlen('000')
voc_label = Label(wri, 100, 100, 'VOC:')
voc_value_label = Label(wri, 100, 127, co2_data_width,
bdcolor=YELLOW)

p25_index_width = wri.stringlen('000.0 ug/m^3')
p25_label = Label(wri, 100, 200, 'P2.5:')
p25_value_label = Label(wri, 100, 230, co2_data_width,
bdcolor=YELLOW)
```

8. We create a method called meter_update, which is used to update the *Meter* class objects. Whenever a new data point for one of the parameters is received, we call this method to set the new value and update the display.

```
def meter_update(meter, update_value):
    meter.value(update_value)
    refresh(ssd)
```

9. Similarly, we create a method called label_update, which is used to update the numerical value of Label class objects.

```
def label_update(label, update_value):
    label.value(update_value)
    refresh(ssd)
```

10. We enter an infinite loop, where we obtain the sensor values and update the display. If the SCD41 sensor data is ready, we scale the data and update the co2_meter object along with the co2_label_ update object. In this case, we are updating the CO2.

```
while scd4x.get_data_ready_status() is False:
    utime.sleep(0.1)
co2, temperature, humidity = scd4x.read_measurement()
scaled_co2 = (co2.co2 - 400) / 4600
meter_update(co2_meter, scaled_co2)
label_update(co2_value_label, "{0} ppm".format(co2.co2))
```

11. Then, we wait for new SEN55 sensor data to become available. We
     retrieve the measured values and update the display with the VOC
     index and PM2.5 concentration values.

```
while sen5x.read_data_ready() is False:
    time.sleep(0.1)

# Read measured values -> clears the "data ready" flag
sen5x_values = sen5x.read_measured_values()
print(sen5x_values)
voc_value = sen5x_values.voc_index.scaled
p25_concentration = sen5x_values.mass_concentration_2p5.physical
p25_update = p25_concentration / 100
voc_update = (voc_value) / 500
meter_update(voc_meter, voc_update)
meter_update(p25_meter, p25_update)
label_update(voc_value_label, "{0}".format(voc_value))
label_update(p25_value_label, "{0}".format(p25_concentration))
```

Due to its length, we chose not to share the complete code sample but made it
available for download along with this chapter as *ch03_visual_aid.py*. When uploaded to
the Adafruit ESP32-S3 and executed, the display looks as shown in Figure 3-23. You can
also save this file as *main.py* on your ESP32-S3 and let it run automatically upon reset.

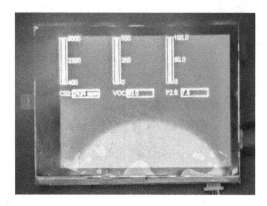

Figure 3-23. *Visual aid in action*

This visual aid is a proof of concept. User interface design is a field of its own. We recommend taking this example and building a rich and colorful display. Consider the following things while designing your visual aid:

- How would you utilize the space available on the display while visualizing the data on your display?

- Parameters that would be useful to your customer

- The display we chose comes with a touchscreen controller. How do you use it to navigate between different screens?

LVGL

LVGL refers to the Light and Versatile Graphics Library. It is an open source framework to design user interfaces on memory-constrained devices like the ESP32-S3 microcontroller. LVGL comes with MicroPython support, and you can read more about it here: `https://docs.lvgl.io/master/details/integration/bindings/micropython.html`. LVGL enables the building of a feature-rich user interface. When writing this chapter, we tried compiling a MicroPython build with the LVGL libraries but couldn't get it working. If we succeed, we will upload our binary alongside the MicroPython binary we shared in Chapter 1.

Challenge

For our visual aid, we used sensor data. Try repeating the same example using the air quality data retrieved using the AirNow API. The AirNow API is rate-limited to 500 requests per hour. So you need to be well under the limit to ensure that you don't violate the terms of the agreement. How would you accomplish this?

Taking Your Visual Aid to Market

So far, we have focused on building our visual aid using the ESP32. Once you have built your prototype, it is time to consider how you would market this product.

Revenue Model

What is the business model for a visual aid? Can you sell the hardware to the customer and remain profitable? Can you generate additional revenue from a recurring subscription? A business model must be established before proceeding with product development.

Product Pricing

What is your product's target cost? This determines its components. For example, if the target cost is under $200, choosing SEN55 and SCD41 sensors for *in situ* data collection is impossible. You may have to forget the sensors and use your database that collects data from a public data source to furnish air quality data to your customers. While estimating the cost of components to set your target cost, assume that the total cost of manufacturing 1 unit would be at least 1.5 times more than your estimated bill of material costs.

Enclosure

The first step in product enclosure design is deciding on its form factor. Will it be a desktop or wall-mounted device? Your enclosure can be machined, 3D printed, or an off-the-shelf part.

Sourcing Components

While sourcing components, determine the lead times and cost of all components. Is there a price break when you purchase components at volume? You must also track whether the product's components are approaching end of life (EOL). Usually, semiconductor vendors issue alerts when a component is approaching its end of life. They also inform their customers of the last buy date. Sometimes, you can find drop-in replacements for "jellybean" components like voltage regulators, transistors, etc.

Manufacturing

A yearly forecast for the number of units required is needed to set up a manufacturing line. This forecast would help determine whether the product will be manufactured in-house or at a third-party location, as well as the fixtures and software needed to test it as it leaves the manufacturing floor.

Device Provisioning

Your product will contain an ESP32 microcontroller. This means it might have to connect to the internet to publish or collect data from the cloud. The customer needs to set up the Wi-Fi credentials for the product. You need a mechanism to make it easy for your customer. You also need to provision the device with credentials for secure cloud communication. This needs to happen at the factory.

Time to Market

The time to market determines your options for your final design. Do you have six months or two years to bring your product to market? If it is six months, you must use off-the-shelf hardware. You can design a custom PCB with all the components in two years. A good rule of thumb would be that it would take twice as long as your estimated completion time. Remember that hardware projects can get quite gnarly, as a simple revision can take a long time. You must try to nail the product specifications before you start the final design.

Servicing

A troubleshooting manual needs to be developed to address field complaints. It would help determine whether a product needs to be replaced and keep a live track of components that fail often. This would feed into a future design iteration, and the warranty period will be determined. The sensors are probably the most sensitive components that require servicing in this visual aid.

Conclusion

This chapter discussed building a visual aid for air quality monitoring. We took two approaches to collecting air quality data. The first one used a public data source that collected data from agencies across North America. We demonstrated how to parse the data retrieved to build your visual aid. We showed how to interface with the SparkFun Air Quality Combo kit and use open source libraries to create a visual aid that tracks the air quality parameters. Finally, we discussed the factors involved in manufacturing and marketing such a product. In the next chapter, we will explore the Bluetooth capabilities of the ESP32-S3.

## CHAPTER 4

Building Bluetooth Products Using ESP32

In this chapter, we will explore the ESP32-S3's Bluetooth capabilities and build low-power sensor nodes that collect and broadcast data from sensors. We will also briefly discuss profiling the power consumption of low-power devices to select a battery.

Bluetooth Low Energy

Bluetooth Low Energy (BLE) is a standard belonging to the Bluetooth family of protocols. BLE is widely used in applications like headsets, speakers, sensors, etc. Bluetooth Low Energy enabled the creation of low-power sensor nodes that can interface with smartphones to collect and upload data to the cloud.

There are two types of BLE devices: peripheral and central. As the name suggests, a peripheral can be a sensor node, audio device, etc. A central device can be a smartphone or an ESP32-S3 module that collects data from the peripheral and uploads it to the cloud. This chapter will discuss building Bluetooth products using the ESP32-S3 as a peripheral or a central Bluetooth device.

BLE on ESP32

The BLE protocol was designed to run wireless sensors off a coin cell or a primary battery for years. The ESP32-S3 supports BLE and is suitable for building peripherals and gateway devices to collect data from peripherals.

© Sai Yamanoor and Srihari Yamanoor 2025
S. Yamanoor and S. Yamanoor, *IoT Product Development Using ESP32 Microcontrollers*,
https://doi.org/10.1007/979-8-8688-1570-6_4

The ESP32-S3 is a perfect fit for remote monitoring IoT applications where the sensor is installed far away from a power source. The ESP32-S3 sensor node can run off a battery. The data can be collected by an ESP32-S3 gateway installed next to a power source. The gateway can continuously scan for sensors and collect data from the individual sensor nodes.

The ESP32-S3 can communicate with BLE peripherals and transmit their data via Wi-Fi. The gateway is responsible for tracking the battery levels of the peripheral nodes, performing firmware updates on the nodes, etc.

Because of their low cost and their availability in the module form factor, ESP32-S3 microcontrollers are suitable for such applications.

Components Required

The following components are needed for the examples discussed in this chapter:

1. 2 x Adafruit Metro ESP32-S3 (24.95 USD)

2. LSM6DS3 sensor breakout board (any breakout board of your choice)

You can choose any sensor for the Bluetooth sensor node.

The sensor chosen for this chapter was selected to demonstrate the Bluetooth capabilities of the ESP32-S3 microcontroller by interfacing with a sensor and transmitting the collected data wirelessly to another device. You can repeat this example with any sensor, provided you have its drivers or know how to write one.

Sensor Integration

This section will discuss integrating the LSM6DS3 sensor to the ESP32-S3 on the Adafruit Metro Development Board. The LSM6DS3 sensor is connected to the development board, as shown in Table 4-1.

Table 4-1. *Pinouts for interfacing LSM6DS3 breakout board to the Adafruit Metro ESP32-S3*

LSM6DS3 Pin	Adafruit Metro ESP32-S3 Pin
3.3V	3.3V
GND	GND
SCL	GPIO48
SDA	GPIO47

Figure 4-1 shows a Fritzing schematic of the connections.

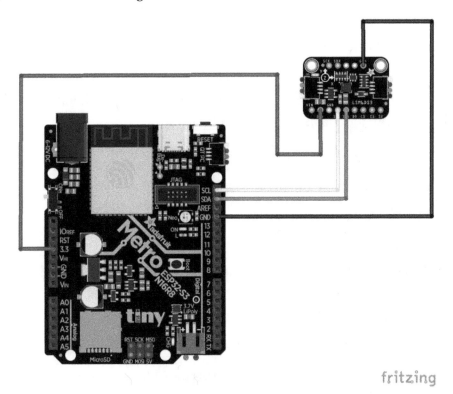

Figure 4-1. *Fritzing schematic to interface LSM6DS3TR breakout with Adafruit Metro ESP32-S3*

Sensor Drivers

The LSM6DS3 sensor drivers are available from Pimoroni under an MIT license. They are available here: https://github.com/pimoroni/lsm6ds3-micropython. We have made them available for download along with this chapter as lsm6sd3.py.

Driver Test

Let's take the driver for a spin and ensure it works.

1. The first step is the essential imports. We will use the I²C interface for our sensor communications, using the I²C class from the machine library.

    ```
    from machine import I2C
    import time
    ```

2. We must also import the LSM6DS3 class from the lsm6ds3 library along with the constant NORMAL_MODE_104HZ.

    ```
    from lsm6ds3 import LSM6DS3, NORMAL_MODE_104HZ
    ```

3. We initialize the I²C interface by setting GPIO 48 as the SCL pin, GPIO 47 as the SDA pin, and the clock frequency to 400 kHz.

    ```
    i2c = I2C(1, scl=48, sda=47, freq=400000)
    ```

4. We use the I²C interface object, i2c, to create an instance of the LSM6DS3 class. We set the data output rate to 104 Hz using the constant NORMAL_MODE_104HZ.

    ```
    lsm6ds3 = LSM6DS3(i2c, mode=NORMAL_MODE_104HZ)
    ```

5. We reset the step count of the LSM6DS3 by calling the reset_step_count method.

    ```
    lsm6ds3.reset_step_count()
    ```

6.   Then, we enter an infinite loop where we retrieve the step count by calling the get_step_count method in a one-second interval.

```
while True:
    steps = lsm6ds3.get_step_count()
    print("Steps: {}".format(steps))
    time.sleep(10)
```

Putting it all together, we have

```
from machine import I2C
import time
from lsm6ds3 import LSM6DS3, NORMAL_MODE_104HZ

i2c = I2C(1, scl=48, sda=47, freq=400000)
lsm6ds3 = LSM6DS3(i2c, mode=NORMAL_MODE_104HZ)

lsm6ds3.reset_step_count()

while True:
    steps = lsm6ds3.get_step_count()
    print("Steps: {}".format(steps))
    time.sleep(10)
```

You can type in the above code sample and run it using the *Run Current Script* button from the Thonny editor (Figure 4-2).

Figure 4-2. *Execute pedometer test code*

When we run the above script, the step count starts printing. Try carrying the unit around for a walk; it should start printing the steps. Giving the breakout board a violent shake should also work! Figure 4-3 shows the LSM6DS3 step count.

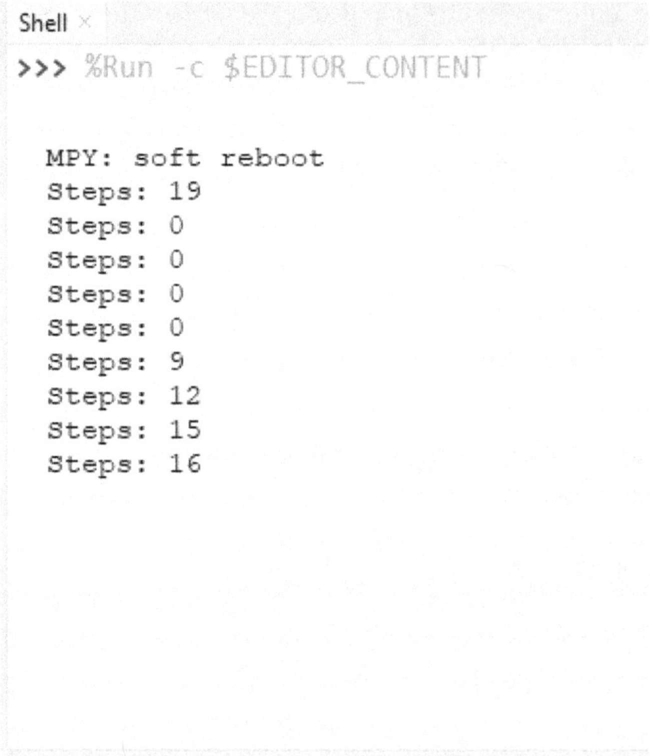

```
Shell ×
>>> %Run -c $EDITOR_CONTENT


  MPY: soft reboot
  Steps: 19
  Steps: 0
  Steps: 0
  Steps: 0
  Steps: 0
  Steps: 9
  Steps: 12
  Steps: 15
  Steps: 16
```

Figure 4-3. *Step counter test*

Next, we will build a Bluetooth-enabled pedometer.

Bluetooth Sensor Node

This section will discuss building a Bluetooth Low Energy (BLE) (peripheral device) pedometer prototype and testing its ability to publish data over Bluetooth and read it using a mobile application. A pedometer could be used as a personal fitness tracker. We get started by installing the prerequisite libraries.

Installing Prerequisite Libraries

This section will install the libraries needed for the examples discussed in this chapter. The only prerequisite is the aioble library. We can install it using the MicroPython package manager, *mip*. mip comes pre-installed with your MicroPython binary if you are running version 1.20 or later. If you are connected to the Wi-Fi network on your development board, the aioble module can be installed as follows:

```
>>> import mip
>>> mip.install("aioble")
```

We made your life easier by creating a script that installs the library for you after connecting to the network. This script is available for download along with this chapter as *ch04_mip_install.py*.

```
import mip
import creds
import network
import time

wifi = network.WLAN(network.STA_IF)
wifi.active(True)
print(wifi.scan())
wifi.connect(creds.SSID, creds.PASSWORD)

while not wifi.isconnected():
    print(".")
    time.sleep(5)

print(f"Success! Connected to {creds.SSID}")
network_params = wifi.ifconfig()
print(f"IP address is {network_params[0]}")

mip.install("aioble")

wifi.disconnect()
wifi.active(False)
```

Running this script from the Thonny IDE should install the aioble library. The installation progress is shown in Figure 4-4.

```
Installing aioble (latest) from https://micropython.org/pi/v2 to /lib
Copying: /lib/aioble/__init__.mpy
Copying: /lib/aioble/core.mpy
Copying: /lib/aioble/device.mpy
Copying: /lib/aioble/peripheral.mpy
Copying: /lib/aioble/server.mpy
Copying: /lib/aioble/central.mpy
Copying: /lib/aioble/client.mpy
Copying: /lib/aioble/l2cap.mpy
Copying: /lib/aioble/security.mpy
Done
```

Figure 4-4. *Installation of the aioble library*

Code Sample Discussion

The code sample discussed in this section is available for download along with this chapter as *ble_pedometer.py*.

The pedometer example discussed in this section is based on the thermometer example available from the MicroPython repository: https://github.com/micropython/micropython/blob/master/examples/bluetooth/ble_temperature.py.

This highlights the ease of building Bluetooth low-energy applications using the examples from the MicroPython repository.

1. We start by importing the requisite libraries and declaring the constants we will use in this example. We will discuss the constants used later in this code.

    ```
    import bluetooth
    from ble_advertising import advertising_payload # used from
    micropython repo
    from micropython import const
    import machine
    import lsm6ds3
    import ustruct
    import utime
    ```

2. We declare the states used in this code sample, namely, *central_connect*, *central_disconnect*, and *indicate_done*. These states are used by the BLE stack's IRQ handler while handling connections to the central device.

```
# ble connection states
central_connect = const(1)
central_disconnect = const(2)
indicate_done = const(20)
```

3. We also declare the constants for the read, notify, and indicate
   operations used to read the step count data from the sensor node.

```
# flags
read_flag = const(0x0002)
notify_flag = const(0x0010)
indicate_flag = const(0x0020)
```

4. Next, we define the Unique Identifiers (UUID) needed for our
   pedometer application. We used the Bluetooth Numbers Database
   repository (https://github.com/NordicSemiconductor/
   bluetooth-numbers-database/tree/master) to determine
   the UUIDs.

```
# org.bluetooth.service.fitness_machine
pedometer_uuid = bluetooth.UUID(0x1826)
# org.bluetooth.characteristic.step_counter_activity.summary
pedometer_characteristic = (
    bluetooth.UUID(0x2B40),
    read_flag | notify_flag | indicate_flag,
)
pedometer_service = (
    pedometer_uuid,
    (pedometer_characteristic,),
)

# org.bluetooth.characteristic.gap.appearance.xml
pedometer_appearance = const(1091)
```

5. In the previous step, we defined the 16-bit UUID for the fitness
   machine service (0x1826) and the step counter characteristic
   (0x2B40). A service is typically a collection of characteristics.
   In this case, the step counter characteristic is a part of the

fitness machine service. We also define the GAP profile for the pedometer. The READ, NOTIFY, and INDICATE flags are enabled. The READ flag enables a mobile application to read the step counter data, while the NOTIFY and INDICATE flags provide regular updates to the mobile application when there is a change in value.

6. Next, we initialize the I²C interface and the LSM6DS3 library.

```
i2c = machine.I2C(1, scl=48, sda=47, freq=400000)
pedometer = lsm6ds3.LSM6DS3(i2c, mode=lsm6ds3.NORMAL_MODE_104HZ)
pedometer.reset_step_count()
```

7. Now, we define the ESP32Pedometer class, which handles all Bluetooth communications.

1. The __init__ method initializes BLE communications and starts advertising as a "step_counter". It also registers the service and characteristic attributes along with the advertising payload.

2. The irq_handler method handles all communication-related callbacks, such as connection, disconnection, and data notification services completed.

3. The set_step_count method writes the pedometer data to the step counter characteristic.

4. Finally, the advertise method advertises the BLE device to other nearby devices.

```
class ESP32Pedometer:
    def __init__(self, ble_connection, name="step-counter"):
        self.ble_conn = ble_connection
        self.ble_conn.active(True)
        self.ble_conn.irq(self.irq_handler)
        ((self.handle,),) = self.ble_conn.gatts_register_
        services((pedometer_service,))
        self.connections = set()
        self.payload = advertising_payload(
            name=name, services=[pedometer_uuid],
            appearance=pedometer_appearance
```

```python
        )
        self.advertise()

    def irq_handler(self, event, data):

        if event == central_connect:
            conn_handle, _, _ = data
            self.connections.add(conn_handle)
        elif event == central_disconnect:
            conn_handle, _, _ = data
            self.connections.remove(conn_handle)
            self.advertise()
        elif event == indicate_done:
            conn_handle, value_handle, status = data

    def set_step_count(self, step_count, notify=False,
    indicate=False):
        self.ble_conn.gatts_write(self.handle, ustruct.
        pack("<h", step_count))
        if notify or indicate:
            for conn_handle in self.connections:
                if notify:
                    self.ble_conn.gatts_notify(conn_handle,
                    self.handle)
                if indicate:
                    self.ble_conn.gatts_indicate(conn_handle,
                    self._handle)

    def advertise(self, interval_us=500000):
        # advertise with 500ms interval
        self.ble_conn.gap_advertise(interval_us, adv_data=self.
        payload)
```

5. In the demo( ) method, we create an instance of the BLE class and pass it on to the ESP32Pedometer class. We enter an infinite loop where we notify the connected device if there is a change in the step value once every ten seconds.

```
def demo():
    ble = bluetooth.BLE()
    step_counter = ESP32Pedometer(ble)

    i = 0

    while True:
        i = (i + 1) % 10
        steps = pedometer.get_step_count()
        print("Steps: {}".format(steps))
        step_counter.set_step_count(steps, notify=(i == 0),
        indicate=False)
        utime.sleep_ms(1000)
```

Putting it together, we have

```
import bluetooth
from ble_advertising import advertising_payload # used from
micropython repo
from micropython import const
import machine
import lsm6ds3
import ustruct
import utime

# ble connection states
central_connect = const(1)
central_disconnect = const(2)
indicate_done = const(20)

# flags
read_flag = const(0x0002)
notify_flag = const(0x0010)
indicate_flag = const(0x0020)
```

```python
# org.bluetooth.service.fitness_machine
pedometer_uuid = bluetooth.UUID(0x1826)
# org.bluetooth.characteristic.step_counter_activity.summary
pedometer_characteristic = (
    bluetooth.UUID(0x2B40),
    read_flag | notify_flag | indicate_flag,
)
pedometer_service = (
    pedometer_uuid,
    (pedometer_characteristic,),
)

# org.bluetooth.characteristic.gap.appearance.xml
pedometer_appearance = const(1091)

i2c = machine.I2C(1, scl=48, sda=47, freq=400000)
pedometer = lsm6ds3.LSM6DS3(i2c, mode=lsm6ds3.NORMAL_MODE_104HZ)

pedometer.reset_step_count()

class ESP32Pedometer:
    def __init__(self, ble_connection, name="step-counter"):
        self.ble_conn = ble_connection
        self.ble_conn.active(True)
        self.ble_conn.irq(self.irq_handler)
        ((self.handle,),) = self.ble_conn.gatts_register_services(
        ((pedometer_service,))
        self.connections = set()
        self.payload = advertising_payload(
            name=name, services=[pedometer_uuid], appearance=pedometer_
            appearance
        )
        self.advertise()

    def irq_handler(self, event, data):

        if event == central_connect:
            conn_handle, _, _ = data
            self.connections.add(conn_handle)
```

```python
        elif event == central_disconnect:
            conn_handle, _, _ = data
            self.connections.remove(conn_handle)
            self.advertise()
        elif event == indicate_done:
            conn_handle, value_handle, status = data

    def set_step_count(self, step_count, notify=False, indicate=False):
        self.ble_conn.gatts_write(self.handle, ustruct.pack("<h",
        step_count))
        if notify or indicate:
            for conn_handle in self.connections:
                if notify:
                    self.ble_conn.gatts_notify(conn_handle, self.handle)
                if indicate:
                    self.ble_conn.gatts_indicate(conn_handle, self._handle)

    def advertise(self, interval_us=500000):
        # advertise with 500ms interval
        self.ble_conn.gap_advertise(interval_us, adv_data=self.payload)

def demo():
    ble = bluetooth.BLE()
    step_counter = ESP32Pedometer(ble)

    i = 0

    while True:
        i = (i + 1) % 10
        steps = pedometer.get_step_count()
        print("Steps: {}".format(steps))
        step_counter.set_step_count(steps, notify=(i == 0), indicate=False)
        utime.sleep_ms(1000)

if __name__ == "__main__":
    demo()
```

You can type in the above code sample and run it using the *Run Current Script* button from the Thonny editor (Figure 4-5).

Figure 4-5. *Execute pedometer test code*

When we run the above script, the step count starts printing. Now, we can try to read the step count data using a mobile application. We recommend using the nRF Connect for Mobile application. It is available for both Android and Apple devices. Let's review reading the step count data using the mobile application.

1. After installing the mobile app, run a scan for nearby devices from the top right corner (Figure 4-6).

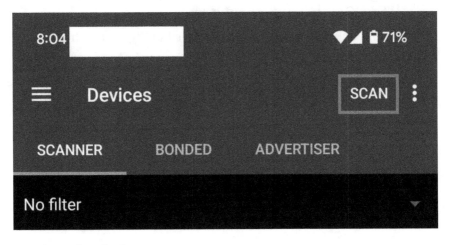

Figure 4-6. *Scan for devices*

2. If the code runs on the ESP32, it should be advertising, and you should be able to spot the step counter as shown in Figure 4-7.

Figure 4-7. *Locate step counters*

133

3. Upon connecting to the step counter, we should be able to review the services available on the connected device (Figure 4-8).

Figure 4-8. *Services available on the connected device*

4. In the snapshot, there is a service called Fitness Machine. Under Fitness Machine, the attributes available under the service are displayed. Click on the notification service highlighted in the red rectangle.

5. You are subscribed for notifications on your pedometer; try walking with it, and you should see an update to the value field highlighted by the yellow rectangle in Figure 4-9. The value field is in little-endian order, i.e., for a 2-byte field, the least significant byte is written at the lower address. In this case, the step count is 0x001B, which is 27 steps. Try walking around and notice the step count update.

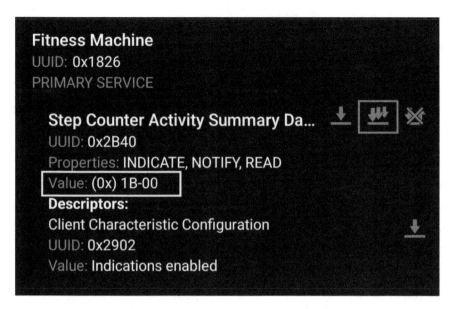

Figure 4-9. *Fitness Machine service*

There you have it! You have built your first ESP32-based Bluetooth application and read the data using a mobile device. This proof of concept is the first step to building a Bluetooth product using the ESP32. A mobile application is necessary to read data from the ESP32 regularly.

On the ESP32, further refinements to the prototype are necessary. This includes the following:

1. Restart the step count every day at midnight.

2. Logging the step count along with the timestamp to local memory. This would let us save data while not connected to the mobile device.

3. Track different physical activities using pace, accelerometer patterns, etc.

A prototype is feasible when it simulates some or all of the product features. As you gather more information from the prototype, your product requirements could change. For example, you can eliminate a requirement or add one. The biggest challenge with hardware products is that when a requirement is altered, or a flaw is identified in the design, it can disrupt the schedule. A good rule of thumb would be to assume that it takes twice as long as you think it takes you to build the first iteration of your product.

135

Now that we have built a proof of concept for collecting data from a sensor using the ESP32, we will next review how we could use another ESP32-S3 to connect to this step counter!

Bluetooth/Wi-Fi Gateway Using ESP32

In this example, we will connect to the pedometer we created in the previous step via Bluetooth using another Adafruit ESP32-S3 Metro and publish the data to a cloud platform via Wi-Fi. The cloud platform we will be using will be Adafruit IO, and we recommend checking out Chapter 2 if you are not familiar with it. We recommend following the instructions provided there to create a feed and a webhook.

This example demonstrates the ESP32's ability to communicate with Bluetooth sensors to aggregate data and publish it through Wi-Fi.

The example discussed in this section is available for download along with this chapter as *ble_pedometer_client.py*. It is based on the temperature sensor client example in the *micropython-lib* repository: https://github.com/micropython/micropython-lib/blob/master/micropython/bluetooth/aioble/examples/temp_client.py.

1. We get started by importing the requisite libraries for this example:

   ```
   import asyncio
   import aioble
   import bluetooth
   import ustruct
   import network
   import utime
   import creds
   import urequests
   ```

2. We define the Unique Identifiers of the pedometer discussed in the previous section.

   ```
   # org.bluetooth.service.fitness_machine
   _FIT_MACHINE_UUID = bluetooth.UUID(0x1826)
   # org.bluetooth.characteristic.step_counter_activity.summary
   _STEP_COUNTER_UUID = bluetooth.UUID(0x2B40)
   ```

3. We also define the IO_FEED_ID needed to publish data to the
    Adafruit IO Feed.

```
IO_FEED_ID = "abcd123456"

parameters = {
    "Content-Type" : "application/json",
}
```

4. We connect to the Wi-Fi network using the credentials stored in
    secrets.py. Refer to previous chapters in case you are familiar with
    secrets.py.

```
wifi = network.WLAN(network.STA_IF)
wifi.active(True)
print(wifi.scan())
wifi.connect(creds.SSID, creds.PASSWORD)

while not wifi.isconnected():
    print(".")
    utime.sleep(1)

print(f"Success! Connected to {creds.SSID}")
network_params = wifi.ifconfig()
print(f"IP address is {network_params[0]}")
```

5. In the pedometer example, we packed the step count in the little-
    endian order. In this example, a helper function is defined to
    unpack the byte array after reading the data from the pedometer.

```
def parse_step_count(data):
    return ustruct.unpack("<h", data)[0]
```

6. Next, we define the method connect_step_counter() that is
    used to scan for pedometer with the name "step-counter" and
    contains the unique identifier that carries the step counter data.

```
async def connect_step_counter():
    async with aioble.scan(5000, interval_us=30000, window_
    us=30000, active=True) as scanner:
```

```
        async for scan_device in scanner:
            # See if it matches our name and the fitnesss machine
              service.
            if scan_device.name() == "step-counter" and _FIT_
            MACHINE_UUID in scan_device.services():
                return scan_device.device
    return None
```

7. Next, we define the `bluetooth_client_task()` where we scan for the pedometer. Upon discovering the pedometer, we connect to it and retrieve the data from the step count characteristic (_STEP_COUNTER_UUID). We also publish the data to Adafruit IO by calling the `post_data()` method. We repeat this block every ten seconds while the ESP32 is connected to the pedometer.

```
async def bluetooth_client_task():
    pedometer = await connect_step_counter()
    if pedometer is None:
        print("Step Counter not found")
        return

    try:
        connection = await pedometer.connect()
    except Exception:
        print("Timeout during connection")
        return

    async with connection:
        try:
            fitness_service = await connection.service
            (_FIT_MACHINE_UUID)
            step_count_rx = await fitness_service.characteristic(_
            STEP_COUNTER_UUID)
        except asyncio.TimeoutError:
            print("Timeout discovering services/characteristics")
            return
```

```
    while connection.is_connected():
        step_count = parse_step_count(await step_count_
        rx.read())
        print("Step Count: {0}".format(step_count))
        post_data(IO_FEED_ID, str(step_count))
        await asyncio.sleep_ms(10000)
```

8. Next, we define the post_data() method that publishes data
    to Adafruit IO. It is identical to the post_id() method from
    Chapter 2.

```
def post_data(feed_id, data):
    url = 'https://io.adafruit.com/api/v2/webhooks/feed/'
    url += feed_id + "/?"
    for key, value in parameters.items():
        url += key + "=" + value + "&"
    url += "value=" + data

    try:
        response = urequests.post(url)
    except Exception as error:
        print(error)
    else:
        if response.status_code == 200:
            print(response.json())
        else:
            print(response.reason)

if __name__ == "__main__":
    asyncio.run(bluetooth_client_task())
```

The complete code sample is available for download along with this chapter.
When we run this script on the second Adafruit Metro ESP32-S3, we can observe the
connection to the pedometer, retrieve data from the step counter characteristic, and
publish it to Adafruit IO (Figure 4-10).

```
IP address is 192.168.1.52
Connecting to Device(ADDR_PUBLIC, ec:da:3b          )
Step Count: 91
{'created_at': '2024-12-26T02:00:06Z', 'id':                        'expiration': '2025-01-25T02:00:06Z',
id': 2973285, 'value': '91', 'feed_key': 'step-count'}
Step Count: 91
{'created_at': '2024-12-26T02:00:17Z', 'id':                        'expiration': '2025-01-25T02:00:17Z',
id': 2973285, 'value': '91', 'feed_key': 'step-count'}
```

Figure 4-10. *Retrieving data from the pedometer*

Take the pedometer for a spin, and you should be able to look at the live feed of the pedometer data on Adafruit IO (as shown in Figure 4-11). If you are not familiar with Adafruit IO feeds, we recommend checking out Chapter 2.

Figure 4-11. *Step count data uploaded to Adafruit IO*

Now that we have reviewed building a Bluetooth sensor node and a gateway using the ESP32-S3, let's take a quick look at power profiling your sensor node.

Power Profiling for Low-Power Applications

When building low-power applications, the most significant decision you need to make is the power source. How will the low-power device be powered? Some options include a battery, supercapacitor, or solar panel. If we use a battery, we must select a battery chemistry suitable for the application. Primary lithium batteries seem more appropriate for outdoor applications as they are rated for temperature fluctuations. Primary lithium battery options are abundant in standard battery sizes in the market. The battery can be sized according to the peak current consumption and the suggested replacement frequency.

For our pedometer application, we can use a rechargeable LiPo battery. This is because pedometers can be recharged by the user on a regular basis. The LiPo battery can be sized based on the peak current consumption and how often we expect the consumer to recharge the pedometer.

In both cases, we need to understand the overall current consumption of the device under design. This includes the peak current consumption as well as the current consumption during sleep. Figure 4-12 shows the current consumption of the pedometer under normal operation.

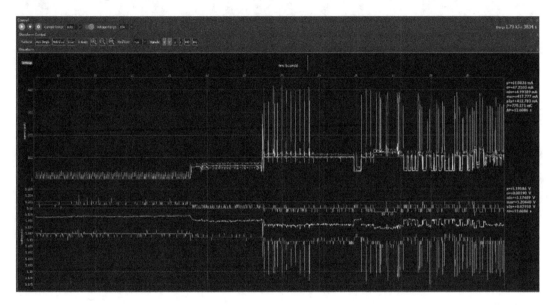

Figure 4-12. *60mA Current Consumption observed during regular operation of the sensor node*

Figure 4-13 shows the pedometer's current consumption during sleep. It is about 1 mA, considered very high because we can achieve sleep current in the order of microamperes. This is because the development board has a lot of bells and whistles that are not needed in the final product including an onboard power LED. A power profiler will help us understand the power consumption of our device and select a battery.

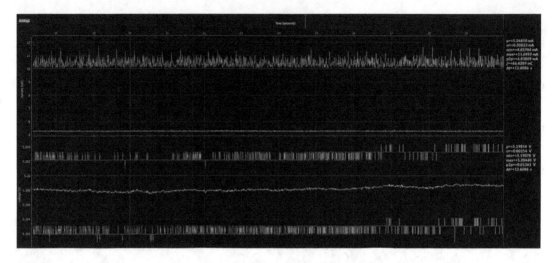

Figure 4-13. *1mA current consumption observed in sleep mode*

Investing in a power profiler tool is essential for product development. There are several profilers in the market. We recommend two options, and you may choose one depending on your budget:

- Nordic Power Profiler Kit II – 100 USD (`https://www.adafruit.com/product/5048`)

- Joulescope JS220 – 999 USD (`https://www.joulescope.com/`)

A power profiler can help identify current leaks in your design and identify areas for improvement.

Conclusion

In this chapter, we reviewed building Bluetooth applications in MicroPython using the ESP32-S3. We started by reviewing a Bluetooth sensor node and then a Bluetooth gateway that reads data from the sensor. In the next chapter, we will work with low-power, long-range radios!

## CHAPTER 5

Low-Power and Long-Range Radios with ESP32

This chapter will explore interfacing low-power radios to the ESP32-S3 microcontroller and their applications. We will discuss the use of long-range radios in IoT products and the role of the ESP32-S3 in developing such products.

LoRa Radios

LoRa refers to Long Range, and LoRa radios are useful in low-power applications such as sensor nodes that run off a battery and stream small payloads of data. LoRa radios are based off a proprietary protocol developed by a company called Semtech. They are especially useful in applications where there is limited access to Wi-Fi. This chapter will discuss interfacing the ESP32-S3 to a LoRa radio and developing applications around it.

Required Components

Table 5-1 shows the components required for the examples discussed in this chapter.

© Sai Yamanoor and Srihari Yamanoor 2025
S. Yamanoor and S. Yamanoor, *IoT Product Development Using ESP32 Microcontrollers*,
https://doi.org/10.1007/979-8-8688-1570-6_5

Table 5-1. *Components used in this chapter*

Item	Description	Quantity	Price (in USD)	Link
1	Adafruit Metro ESP32-S3	2	24.95	`https://www.adafruit.com/product/5500`
2	Adafruit RFM95W LoRa Radio Transceiver Breakout	2	19.95	`https://www.adafruit.com/product/3072`
3	SMA Connector for 1.6mm PCBs	2	2.50	`https://www.adafruit.com/product/1865`
4	915MHz LoRa Antenna set	1	9.99	`https://www.amazon.com/dp/B0CTXL61LY`
5	Jumper wire set	1	6.98	`https://www.amazon.com/dp/B07GD2BWPY`
6	Any sensor of your choice	1	NA	NA

Interfacing LoRa Radios to ESP32-S3

This section will discuss interfacing LoRa radios to the ESP32-S3 microcontroller. We will specifically interface the Adafruit RFM95W MHz breakout to the Adafruit Metro ESP32-S3. Then, we will transmit messages from one radio to another.

Library Installation

The library required for the examples in this section is the `lora` library from the MicroPython package index. We can install it using the MicroPython package manager, *mip*. We have extensively discussed MicroPython package installation in previous chapters (see Chapters 2 and 4). We made your life easier by creating a script that installs the library for you after connecting to the network. This script is available for download along with this chapter as *ch05_lora_install.py*.

Running this script from the Thonny IDE should install the `lora` library. The installation progress is shown in Figure 5-1.

```
Installing lora (latest) from https://micropython.org/pi/v2 to /lib
Copying: /lib/lora/__init__.mpy
Copying: /lib/lora/modem.mpy
Done
Installing lora-async (latest) from https://micropython.org/pi/v2 to /lib
Exists: /lib/lora/__init__.mpy
Exists: /lib/lora/modem.mpy
Copying: /lib/lora/async_modem.mpy
Done
Installing lora-sx127x (latest) from https://micropython.org/pi/v2 to /lib
Exists: /lib/lora/__init__.mpy
Exists: /lib/lora/modem.mpy
Copying: /lib/lora/sx127x.mpy
Done
```

Figure 5-1. *Installation of the lora library*

Now that we have installed the required libraries, let's wire up the RFM95W breakout to the Adafruit Metro ESP32-S3.

Antenna Assembly

The RFM95W breakout board requires some assembly. This includes the header pins for the breakout board and the SMA antenna connector. Figure 5-2 shows a fully assembled breakout board (including its antenna) onto a breadboard.

Figure 5-2. *Assembled RFM95W breakout board*

If you don't necessarily have soldering experience, we recommend this excellent tutorial from Adafruit on soldering and assembling the board. This includes the SMA connector for the radio antenna: `https://learn.adafruit.com/adafruit-rfm69hcw-and-rfm96-rfm95-rfm98-lora-packet-padio-breakouts/assembly`.

Wiring Up the RFM95W Breakout

The RFM95W breakout is wired to the Adafruit Metro ESP32-S3, as listed in Table 5-2.

Table 5-2. *Interfacing the ESP32 to the RFM95W*

ESP32 Pin	RFM95W Pin
VHI	VIN
GND	GND
D8	G0
D9	RST
D10	CS
D11	MOSI
D12	MISO
D13	SCK

Figure 5-3 shows a breadboard schematic to connect the RFM95W breakout to the Adafruit Metro ESP32-S3.

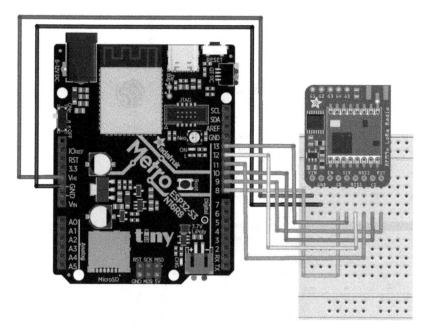

Figure 5-3. *Fritzing schematic for interfacing RFM95W breakout to the Adafruit Metro ESP32-S3*

A fully assembled and wired-up setup looks like the one shown in Figure 5-4.

Figure 5-4. *Fully assembled RFM95W breakout interfaced to the Adafruit Metro ESP32-S3*

Once you wire up both the Adafruit Metro ESP32-S3 boards and the RFM95W breakout boards, it is time to take them for a spin with a spin code sample.

Testing the Breakout Board

Let's test whether the breakout board's wiring is correct by running a simple example. This example was adapted from https://github.com/micropython/micropython-lib/blob/master/micropython/lora/examples/simple_rxtx/simple_rxtx.py. It is available under an MIT license.

The modified code sample is available for download along with this chapter as *ch05_lora_test_example.py*.

This example will discuss transmitting and receiving messages using LoRa transceivers. Let's get started:

1. We get started by importing the requisite libraries.

    ```
    import time
    from machine import Pin, SPI
    from lora.sx127x import SX1276
    ```

2. We define the method get_modem() where we define the
   communication parameters. In the United States, the ISM band
   (Industrial, Scientific, and Medical Band) is 902–928 MHz. We use
   the default parameters for the rest of them and define a dictionary
   as follows:

```
lora_cfg = {
    "freq_khz": 916000,
    "sf": 8,
    "bw": "500",   # kHz
    "coding_rate": 8,
    "preamble_len": 12,
    "output_power": 0,   # dBm
}
```

If you are experiencing issues with the radio range, you can adjust the output
power to a maximum of +20 dBm.

---

3. The LoRa module is equipped with an SPI interface. So we
   initialize the SPI interface and create an instance of the SX1276
   class from the lora library. The pins were initialized according to
   the connections made earlier.

```
return SX1276(
    spi=SPI(1, baudrate=2000_000, polarity=0, phase=0,
            miso=Pin(12), mosi=Pin(11), sck=Pin(13)),
    cs=Pin(10),
    dio0=Pin(8),
    reset=Pin(9),
    lora_cfg=lora_cfg,
)
```

4. Next, we define our `main()` function, which involves transmitting and receiving messages between the two modems. We get started by initializing the SX1276 module by calling the `get_modem()` method discussed in the previous step.

```
print("Initializing...")
modem = get_modem()
```

5. We initialize the `counter` variable before entering an infinite while loop. In the loop, we call the `send()` method to transmit a "Hello World" message to the other radio.

```
print("Sending...")
modem.send(f"Hello world #{counter}".encode())
```

6. Next, we read incoming messages by calling the `recv()` method. Because the method awaits incoming messages, we set a maximum timeout of `5000 milliseconds`. If there is a message, we print it out. If not, we print `Timeout`.

```
print("Receiving...")
rx = modem.recv(timeout_ms=5000)
if rx:
    print(f"Received: {rx!r}")
else:
    print("Timeout!")
```

7. We increment the `counter` variable and repeat from the top after a two-second delay.

```
time.sleep(2)
counter += 1
```

Putting it all together, we have

```
# MicroPython lora simple_rxtx example - synchronous API version
# MIT license; Copyright (c) 2023 Angus Gratton
import time
from machine import Pin, SPI
from lora.sx127x import SX1276
```

```python
def get_modem():

    lora_cfg = {
        "freq_khz": 916000,
        "sf": 8,
        "bw": "500",   # kHz
        "coding_rate": 8,
        "preamble_len": 12,
        "output_power": 0,   # dBm
    }

    return SX1276(
        spi=SPI(1, baudrate=2000_000, polarity=0, phase=0,
                miso=Pin(12), mosi=Pin(11), sck=Pin(13)),
        cs=Pin(10),
        dio0=Pin(8),
        reset=Pin(9),
        lora_cfg=lora_cfg,
    )

def main():
    print("Initializing...")
    modem = get_modem()

    counter = 0
    while True:
        print("Sending...")
        modem.send(f"Hello world #{counter}".encode())

        print("Receiving...")
        rx = modem.recv(timeout_ms=5000)
        if rx:
            print(f"Received: {rx!r}")
        else:
            print("Timeout!")
        time.sleep(2)
        counter += 1

if __name__ == "__main__":
    main()
```

In order to test the code sample, we need to save them on both the Adafruit Metro ESP32-S3 boards as *main.py*. When we rest the boards and monitor their corresponding serial ports, we should see the output shown in Figure 5-5.

```
Shell
  Receiving...
  Received: RxPacket(b'Hello world from MicroPython #6', 61280, -45, -104, True)
  Sending...
  Receiving...
  Received: RxPacket(b'Hello world from MicroPython #7', 65390, -47, -103, True)
  Sending...
  Receiving...
  Received: RxPacket(b'Hello world from MicroPython #8', 69507, -51, -104, True)
  Sending...
  Receiving...
  Received: RxPacket(b'Hello wob\x0cd from MicroPython #9', 73618, -51, -103, True)
  Sending...
  Receiving...
  Received: RxPacket(b'Hello world from MicroPython #10', 77730, -48, -103, True)
  Sending...
  Receiving...
  Received: RxPacket(b'Hello world from MicroPython #11', 81840, -47, -104, True)
```

Figure 5-5. *Transmitting and receiving messages between two Adafruit ESP32-S3 boards*

Now that we know the boards are working, we will review the transmission of sensor data from one board to another, which will publish the data to the cloud.

Sensor Data Aggregation and Publishing to the Cloud

Now that we know that the radios are working, we will collect temperature sensor data using one Adafruit Metro ESP32-S3 and transmit it to the other LoRa radio.

Purpose

This example highlights scenarios where the sensor is installed outside the Wi-Fi range. We could use one ESP32 microcontroller to collect sensor data in such cases. We can install another ESP32 microcontroller within the Wi-Fi range. This one acts as a gateway responsible for aggregating sensor data from all sensor nodes and publishing the data to the cloud.

ESP32 LoRa Sensor Node Example

First, we will review the code sample for transmitting sensor data to another LoRa radio. For this example, you can use any sensor, but we chose the *LSM6DS3* sensor discussed in the previous chapter. The drivers for this sensor are available from Pimoroni under an MIT license. We have made it available with downloads from the previous chapter.

The example discussed in this section is available for download along with this chapter as *ch05_lora_sensor_node_example.py*.

1. We get started with the imports required for this example.

```
import utime
from machine import Pin, SPI, I2C
from lora.sx127x import SX1276
from lsm6ds3 import LSM6DS3, NORMAL_MODE_104HZ
```

2. We define the init_imu() function to initialize the LSM6DS3 sensor. In this method, we make use of the LSM6DS3 class to initialize the IMU via the I²C interface.

```
def init_imu():
    i2c = I2C(0, scl=48, sda=47)
    return LSM6DS3(i2c, mode=NORMAL_MODE_104HZ)
```

3. We reuse the get_modem() function discussed in the previous section:

```
def get_modem():
    lora_cfg = {
        "freq_khz": 916000,
        "sf": 8,
        "bw": "500",  # kHz
        "coding_rate": 8,
        "preamble_len": 12,
        "output_power": 0,  # dBm
    }

    return SX1276(
        spi=SPI(1, baudrate=2000_000, polarity=0, phase=0,
                miso=Pin(12), mosi=Pin(11), sck=Pin(13)),
        cs=Pin(10),
        dio0=Pin(8),
        reset=Pin(9),
        lora_cfg=lora_cfg,
    )
```

If you are experiencing issues with the radio range, you can adjust the output power in lora_cfg to a maximum of +20 dBm.

4. In our main() function, after initializing the sensor and modem discussed in the previous steps, we enter a while loop. In the while loop, we retrieve the step count from the IMU. Then, we transmit the step count to the other LoRa radio using the modem object's send() method.

```python
def main():
    modem = get_modem()
    imu = init_imu()

    while True:
        steps = imu.get_step_count()
        print("Steps = {}".format(steps))
        modem.send("Steps:{}".format(steps))
        utime.sleep(10)
```

5. Putting it all together, we have

```python
import utime
from machine import Pin, SPI, I2C
from lora.sx127x import SX1276
from lsm6ds3 import LSM6DS3, NORMAL_MODE_104HZ

def init_imu():
    i2c = I2C(0, scl=48, sda=47)
    return LSM6DS3(i2c, mode=NORMAL_MODE_104HZ)

def get_modem():
    lora_cfg = {
        "freq_khz": 916000,
        "sf": 8,
        "bw": "500",   # kHz
```

```
        "coding_rate": 8,
        "preamble_len": 12,
        "output_power": 0,  # dBm
    }

    return SX1276(
        spi=SPI(1, baudrate=2000_000, polarity=0, phase=0,
                miso=Pin(12), mosi=Pin(11), sck=Pin(13)),
        cs=Pin(10),
        dio0=Pin(8),
        reset=Pin(9),
        lora_cfg=lora_cfg,
    )

def main():
    modem = get_modem()
    imu = init_imu()

    while True:
        steps = imu.get_step_count()
        print("Steps = {}".format(steps))
        modem.send("Steps:{}".format(steps))
        utime.sleep(10)

if __name__ == "__main__":
    main()
```

When we save the code sample to the Adafruit Metro ESP32-S3 as *main.py* and run it, we get the output shown in Figure 5-6.

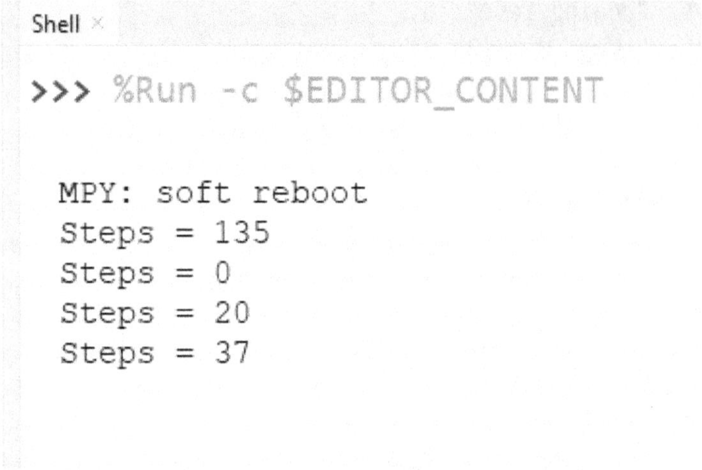

```
Shell ×

>>> %Run -c $EDITOR_CONTENT


MPY: soft reboot
Steps = 135
Steps = 0
Steps = 20
Steps = 37
```

Figure 5-6. *LoRa sensor node*

Now that the sensor node is transmitting, we will review the gateway example where the ESP32 collects the sensor data from the LoRa radio and publishes it to the cloud.

ESP32 LoRa Gateway Example

In this gateway example, we will discuss reading and publishing the sensor data to the Adafruit IO service.

You might have noticed that we have used the Adafruit IO service across chapters when we want to publish data to the cloud. This is to demonstrate that data can be published securely to any cloud service. You can use this example to publish data to any cloud service.

The example discussed in this section is available for download along with this chapter as *ch05_lora_gateway_example.py*.

1. We get started by importing the libraries required for this example:

```
import utime
import network
import secrets
from lora.sx127x import SX1276
```

```
from machine import Pin, SPI
import network
import urequests
```

2. We declare the constants needed to publish data to the Adafruit IO service. You can review Chapter 2's instructions for creating a feed ID.

```
IO_FEED_ID = "ADAFRUIT_FEED_ID"

parameters = {
    "Content-Type" : "application/json",
}
```

3. Next, we connect to the Wi-Fi network using the credentials stored in secrets.py (we have discussed secrets.py extensively in previous chapters).

```
wlan = network.WLAN(network.STA_IF)
wlan.active(True)
wlan.connect(secrets.SSID, secrets.PASSWORD)

while not wlan.isconnected():
    print(".")
    utime.sleep(1)

print(f"Success! Connected to {secrets.SSID}")
network_params = wlan.ifconfig()
print(f"IP address is {network_params[0]}")
```

4. We reuse the post_data() function from Chapter 4 to publish data to the Adafruit IO service. We also reuse the get_modem() function from the sensor node example.

```
def post_data(feed_id, data):
    url = 'https://io.adafruit.com/api/v2/webhooks/feed/'
    url += feed_id + "/?"
    for key, value in parameters.items():
        url += key + "=" + value + "&"
    url += "value=" + data
```

```python
        try:
            response = urequests.post(url)
        except Exception as error:
            print(error)
        else:
            if response.status_code == 200:
                print(response.json())
            else:
                print(response.reason)

    def get_modem():
        lora_cfg = {
            "freq_khz": 916000,
            "sf": 8,
            "bw": "500",   # kHz
            "coding_rate": 8,
            "preamble_len": 12,
            "output_power": 0,   # dBm
        }

        return SX1276(
            spi=SPI(1, baudrate=2000_000, polarity=0, phase=0,
                    miso=Pin(12), mosi=Pin(11), sck=Pin(13)),
            cs=Pin(10),
            dio0=Pin(8),
            reset=Pin(9),
            lora_cfg=lora_cfg,
        )
```

If you are experiencing issues with the radio range, you can adjust the output power in lora_cfg to a maximum of +20 dBm.

---

5. In the main function, we initialize the modem and enter the while
    loop, where we read the message from the other LoRa radio with
    a 10,000 millisecond timeout. If the message read is valid, we
    decode the message from the sensor node and parse it to extract
    the step count data. If the payload contains valid data, we publish
    it to the cloud.

```python
def main():
    modem = get_modem()
    while True:
        rx_message = modem.recv(timeout_ms=10000)
        if rx_message:
            message = rx_message.decode("utf-8")
            if "Steps:" in message:
                idx = message.index(":")
                steps = int(message[idx+1:])
                if steps >= 0:
                    post_data(IO_FEED_ID, str(steps))
```

6. Putting it all together, we have

```python
import utime
import network
import secrets
from lora.sx127x import SX1276
from machine import Pin, SPI
import network
import urequests

IO_FEED_ID = "gXT3GmsDGuzkuZfF1Hg8M4jYpYa5"

parameters = {
    "Content-Type" : "application/json",
}

wlan = network.WLAN(network.STA_IF)
wlan.active(True)
wlan.connect(secrets.SSID, secrets.PASSWORD)
```

```python
    while not wlan.isconnected():
        print(".")
        utime.sleep(1)

    print(f"Success! Connected to {secrets.SSID}")
    network_params = wlan.ifconfig()
    print(f"IP address is {network_params[0]}")

    def post_data(feed_id, data):
        url = 'https://io.adafruit.com/api/v2/webhooks/feed/'
        url += feed_id + "/?"
        for key, value in parameters.items():
            url += key + "=" + value + "&"
        url += "value=" + data

        try:
            response = urequests.post(url)
        except Exception as error:
            print(error)
        else:
            if response.status_code == 200:
                print(response.json())
            else:
                print(response.reason)

    def get_modem():
        lora_cfg = {
            "freq_khz": 916000,
            "sf": 8,
            "bw": "500",  # kHz
            "coding_rate": 8,
            "preamble_len": 12,
            "output_power": 0,  # dBm
        }

        return SX1276(
            spi=SPI(1, baudrate=2000_000, polarity=0, phase=0,
                    miso=Pin(12), mosi=Pin(11), sck=Pin(13)),
```

```
            cs=Pin(10),
            dio0=Pin(8),
            reset=Pin(9),
            lora_cfg=lora_cfg,
        )

    def main():
        modem = get_modem()
        while True:
            rx_message = modem.recv(timeout_ms=10000)
            if rx_message:
                message = rx_message.decode("utf-8")
                if "Steps:" in message:
                    idx = message.index(":")
                    steps = int(message[idx+1:])
                    if steps >= 0:
                        post_data(IO_FEED_ID, str(steps))

    if __name__ == "__main__":
        main()
```

When we save the above code sample as main.py and run it on the second Adafruit Metro ESP32-S3 board, we should see an output like that shown in Figure 5-7. This example also assumes that you have the sensor node example running on the first board.

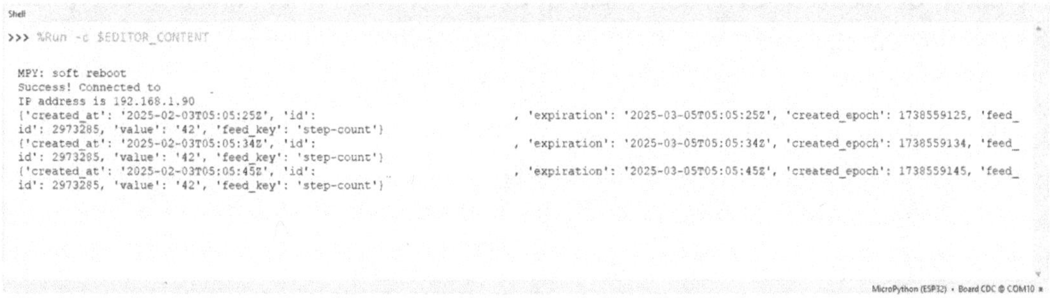

Figure 5-7. *Data uploaded from the gateway to the cloud*

In this example, we discussed collecting sensor data from one sensor and publishing it to the cloud. When you are building products, there are a few other considerations. They are as follows:

- In this example, the communication was all one way, i.e., Sensor ➤ Gateway ➤ Cloud. While this is a proof of concept, your application might require that the cloud can send commands to the gateway to configure the sensor node. This configuration update can include changes to the sensor data report interval, sensor node identification, etc. We demonstrated transmitting messages between the gateways and the sensor nodes. This should aid implementing a mechanism for the sensor node to respond to commands from the gateway.

- While building a product, it can be cheaper to develop the sensor node and the gateway on the same hardware and software platform. In this chapter, we demonstrated that both of them can run identical code on identical hardware. While developing a product, you can write code where you read the GPIO pin state to determine whether a piece of hardware is going to act as a gateway or a sensor node.

Publishing Data to LoRaWAN Networks

LoRaWAN networks refer to Long Range Wide Area Network. They are designed for low-power devices such as an ESP32 sensor node to connect to a public network to publish data. An example of a LoRaWAN network is the Things Network (`https://www.thethingsnetwork.org/`). The Things Network is a community-driven public LoRa network that enables you to connect your low-power device to the cloud. If you are lucky, you might currently reside in a city with a public LoRa network. A heatmap of networks is available (shown in Figure 5-8) from `https://ttnmapper.org/heatmap/`.

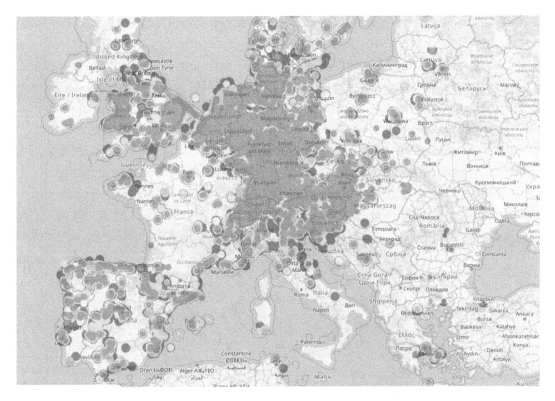

Figure 5-8. *Heatmap of LoRa networks in Europe*

While public LoRa networks were available in our general vicinity in the United States, we could not connect to them. We suspect this was because we were beyond the gateway's range capabilities. If you think your city has a strong LoRa network, we recommend checking out this LoRaWAN library available under an MIT license: `https://github.com/fantasticdonkey/uLoRa`.

Deploying your own private networks is an option when developing a product for a region without public LoRaWAN networks. The price point of deploying your own network can be very steep, and we recommend checking out various options available here: `https://www.thethingsnetwork.org/docs/gateways/`. There are also licensing costs associated with deploying your own network.

Interfacing Cellular Modules to the ESP32

Cellular modules enable connecting your ESP32 to a cellular network. This is especially useful when your devices cannot connect to your customer's Wi-Fi network. Your ESP32 can aggregate sensor data and publish data through a cellular network. The cellular radio that is easiest to interface with an ESP32 is the Notecard Cellular Module (shown in Figure 5-9) from `https://blues.com`. These cellular radios can communicate with an ESP32 via the I²C interface. The folks at Blues have also made a Python library available at `https://github.com/blues/note-python` under an MIT license. They have also provided examples of devices running MicroPython. A Blues Notecard module costs 45 USD and comes with 500 MB of data and ten years of subscription. But there are additional costs associated with routing data from their cloud services to your own cloud services. You can learn more about the Blues Cellular module from `https://shop.blues.com/products/notecard-cellular`. The Notecard Cellular Module comes with certifications required for use in several countries around the world.

Figure 5-9. *Notecard Cellular Module*

Compliance Engineering

The various radio modules we have discussed so far come with regulatory certification for different countries worldwide. But they are restricted to that particular module. If you develop a product where you are combining two radios, for example, a board that contains an ESP32 module and a LoRa module, they might have to go through an additional certification process depending on their intended use. You will need to work with a compliance engineering expert who can recommend the best option for your product.

You are required to go through a self-certification process even when you are designing a product that has a single pre-certified radio.

Conclusion

In this chapter, we discussed interfacing the ESP32 to LoRa radios. We discussed two examples where we interfaced the RFM95W to an Adafruit Metro ESP32-S3. In the examples, we discussed exchanging messages between two radios as well as publishing data from sensor nodes using the ESP32 as a gateway. We also briefly discussed interfacing cellular modules to the ESP32.

CHAPTER 6

Building TinyML Products

This chapter will review the development of TinyML applications using ESP32. We will discuss the purpose of TinyML, its applications in IoT products, and the toolsets available to build TinyML products.

What Is TinyML?

TinyML (Tiny Machine Learning) refers to the ability to make decisions or infer events on a microcontroller like the ESP32. Since the ESP32 microcontroller is very constrained in its memory resources compared to a GPU (Graphics Processing Unit), running machine learning applications (which usually require a GPU) on an ESP32 microcontroller is impossible. TinyML is a framework that provides toolsets to convert machine learning models to run on a microcontroller. Some examples of TinyML applications include anomaly detection, gesture recognition, etc.

This chapter explores the powerful features of the ESP32-S3 microcontroller and their applications in TinyML, edge computing, etc. So we make use of development kits other than the Adafruit Metro ESP32-S3 development kit in this chapter. This is also the only chapter where we don't use MicroPython in code samples.

Need for TinyML

Let's consider a remote monitoring IoT application where we are collecting data from pressure sensors using an ESP32 microcontroller. The pressure sensors are measuring the pressure of gas supply lines connected to a manifold. There are three sensors that wirelessly transmit the measured pressure to an ESP32 gateway.

© Sai Yamanoor and Srihari Yamanoor 2025
S. Yamanoor and S. Yamanoor, *IoT Product Development Using ESP32 Microcontrollers*,
https://doi.org/10.1007/979-8-8688-1570-6_6

The gateway aggregates all the data and uploads it to the cloud. In a typical remote monitoring application (illustrated in Figure 6-1), we develop a machine learning model to run in the cloud to detect anomalies in the collected data. The anomalies could include a drop in pressure pointing to a leak in the system or a sudden increase in consumption. Such inferences could help increase revenues for the organization by sending more supplies to the customer to keep their business operational. This also allows us to generate a forecast of the customer's future needs.

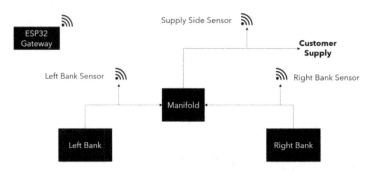

Figure 6-1. *Remote monitoring application example*

This remote monitoring application is scalable when the number of gateways in the fleet is in the order of 100s and the wireless sensor nodes are in the range of 1000s. There are a few challenges when this application scales exponentially. Consider a scenario where we add 100 sensor nodes to each gateway and add a gateway at upwards of 10,000 customer locations worldwide. Such an application presents a few challenges. They are as follows.

The cost associated with uploading every sensor data point to the cloud. These costs include network connectivity, cloud infrastructure, and other related expenses.

The customer might not want their data leaving their premises. In this case, installing a GPU at each customer location is impractical as it increases capital expenditure while scaling the application.

Depending on the data point uploaded, the processing time required to infer the anomaly can be significant. Consider a scenario where a fleet of ESP32 devices is transmitting images to the cloud. The cloud has a pipeline of images to be processed and executes commands after processing each image. There is a delay in responding to the situation, and a backlog in processing the images may occur, depending on the fleet size. TinyML can be used to mitigate the backlog by performing the inference onsite using the ESP32 and only uploading the results alongside the image if necessary. This helps reduce the latency in reaction to an event and decentralizes the processing capabilities.

In these cases, TinyML can help reduce costs. As shown in Figure 6-2, the ESP32 could detect any anomaly and react to a situation immediately. This reaction could shut off any valve or send an alert to order more gas supplies for the customer.

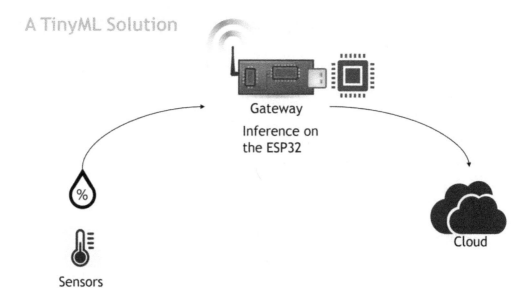

Figure 6-2. *TinyML solution*

There are several advantages to the TinyML approach. They include

- **Reduction in reaction times:** The gateway can immediately react to an anomaly. This is helpful in scenarios where there is poor connectivity

- **Simplifying cloud infrastructure:** We don't have to upload every single data point to the cloud. We only report critical events to the cloud. This helps reduce scaling costs when the application grows exponentially.

- **Data retention:** We only upload data points permitted by the customer.

- **Cost savings:** If an anomaly could be detected using a microcontroller that costs around $1, it can generate significant savings over time.

Developing a TinyML Application

How is a TinyML-enabled IoT application developed? Let's take an IoT application and review how TinyML could be used to enhance it. In this scenario, we will utilize the pressure sensor example discussed earlier. The entire sequence is illustrated in Figure 6-3.

- **Device deployment:** In this phase, IoT devices are deployed in the field and used to collect pressure sensor data using the ESP32. We are deploying ESP32-enabled products connected to pressure sensors. This phase involves bringing the devices online and ensuring that the sensors are reporting valid data.

- **Data collection:** In this phase, we collect sensor data and upload all data points to the cloud. We also iron out any issues in the data collection.

- **Data analysis and labeling:** During the analysis phase, we identify useful features to track and anomalies that are easily detectable using the limited memory resources available on the ESP32. We correlate the sensor data to actual events reported by the customer. For example, a sudden pressure drop could indicate that a valve was fully opened, or a gradual drop overnight could indicate leaks in the system. We confer with the customer to gain a better understanding of the incoming sensor streams.

- **Building and training the model:** Once we have a good understanding of the dataset, we split the data into three sets: training, validation, and testing. We need to ensure that the three datasets represent all the scenarios identified in the previous phase. Then, we build and train a model to interpret the sensor data and identify anomalies. This is an iterative process where we fine-tune the performance of our machine learning model.

- **Model deployment on ESP32:** We convert the model into a format suitable for ESP32 microcontrollers. This process is called quantization. The quantized model is then deployed to the ESP32 gateway. We detect anomalies and other events locally on the gateway. For every anomaly detected, we uploaded the raw data and the result to the cloud. This is to better understand the performance of the quantized model and the results.

- **Refinement:** In this step, the results obtained from the model deployed on the ESP32 gateway are compared to those obtained from the cloud. The model is refined and repeated from step 3 until the results are satisfactory.

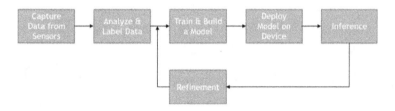

Figure 6-3. *Developing a TinyML application*

In this example, we had to build a model by deploying devices to the field and collecting data. There are datasets for certain applications, such as bearing wear and tear. This provides a good starting point for developing applications, such as critical component health monitoring in turbines. For monitoring the health of a bearing, we can use an accelerometer and a microphone to detect unusual noises or vibrations emanating from the turbine. The ESP32 could detect such anomalies using a model running on it and report them wirelessly to a local gateway. The gateway notifies the cloud to generate a preventative maintenance alert.

This is a great way to prevent equipment downtime by utilizing the ESP32 to detect such issues.

Now that we have discussed the TinyML application development process, we will discuss the toolsets available for developing TinyML applications on the ESP32.

TinyML Toolsets

The TinyML toolsets discussed in this section short-circuit the development process by providing a pre-trained model for an application that already shares similarities with our potential application. Pre-trained models are available to detect keywords in an audio sample, identify objects in a captured image, or detect falls from an accelerometer sample window. A pre-trained model is a good place to get started for any application development. We came across the following toolsets for TinyML application development on ESP32 microcontrollers:

- **TensorFlow Lite for ESP32 Microcontrollers:** This is an official toolset from Espressif for ESP32 microcontrollers. It is available here: `https://github.com/espressif/esp-tflite-micro.git`

- **TensorFlow MicroPython Examples:** The examples provided failed continuous integration tests when this chapter was written. This toolset is available here: `https://github.com/mocleiri/tensorflow-micropython-examples.git`

- **Edge Impulse:** Edge Impulse is an organization that helps engineers build TinyML-enabled IoT products. They provide pre-trained models for a variety of applications and datasets. One can use their pre-trained models to customize it for their application with relative ease. While the evaluation of the tool is free, Edge Impulse requires purchasing a license when you take your product to the market. You can read more about Edge Impulse here: `https://edgeimpulse.com/`

Image Classification Example Using Edge Impulse

In this section, we will discuss how to perform image classification using ESP32. We hope you are familiar with the game of tic-tac-toe (also known as noughts and crosses). We will be building a simple application that can distinguish between the "X" and the "O" pieces of the tic-tac-toe game board.

Hardware Requirements

Table 6-1 shows the hardware required for the example discussed in this chapter.

Table 6-1. *Components used in this example*

Item	Description	Quantity	Price (in USD)	Link
1	ESP32-CAM	1	14.99	`https://www.amazon.com/ESP32-CAM-Development-Bluetooth-Low-Power-Compatible/dp/BODN64QQ54`
2	USB serial adapter	1	9.95	`https://www.adafruit.com/product/954`
3	32GB MicroSD card with adapter	1	NA	Any vendor of your choice

We chose the ESP32-CAM module (shown in Figure 6-4) to show that it is possible to develop TinyML applications using any microcontroller from the ESP32 family. In the next section, we will discuss an application using the Adafruit Metro ESP32-S3.

Figure 6-4. *ESP32-CAM module*

We also need a tic-tac-toe game board like `https://www.amazon.com/dp/BOB2JZHQ2P`. We are just using the game pieces from the board for this example. Any two distinct objects should work for this example.

We will be using a pre-trained model from Edge Impulse and training the model on the dataset we are going to create to distinguish between "X" and "O". Then, we will deploy the quantized model onto the ESP32 and test it.

Building the Dataset

To build our application, an Edge Impulse account is required. You can sign up for a free developer account at `https://edgeimpulse.com/`.

We can build the dataset by capturing images using a mobile phone. Let's get started.

1. After signing up for an Edge Impulse account, the first step is to create a new project. A new project can be created from the landing page of your Edge Impulse account (Figure 6-5).

Figure 6-5. *Create New Edge Impulse*

2. Give a name to your project and configure the project settings (Figure 6-6).

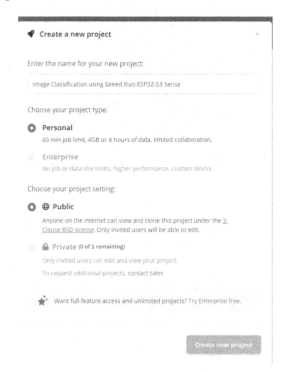

Figure 6-6. *Name the project and configure its settings*

3. It is now time to collect data for our application. We can collect data from our project application dashboard (Figure 6-7).

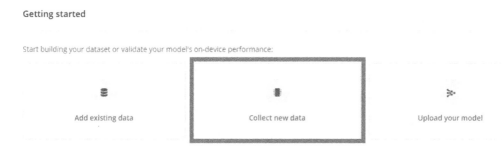

Figure 6-7. *Collect new data*

4. In the next pop-up window, a QR code pops up. In Figure 6-8, the QR code is concealed for privacy reasons. To capture and upload images to the dataset, we scan the QR code using a mobile phone.

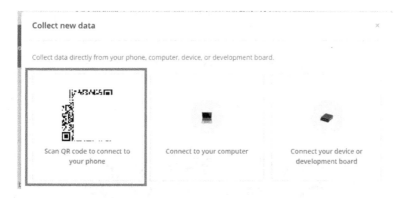

Figure 6-8. *Scan QR code to upload images to the dataset*

5. We connect the phone by scanning the QR code and clicking *Collecting images* (Figure 6-9).

Figure 6-9. *Collecting images using a mobile phone*

6. We grant access to the camera to start taking pictures
    (Figure 6-10).

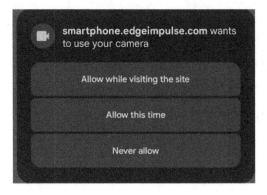

Figure 6-10. *Grant access to the camera*

7. We start taking pictures of the X and O pieces by creating labels as
    shown in Figure 6-11.

Figure 6-11. *Capture images using labels*

8. We will capture images with three classes of labels, namely,
    Nought, Cross, and Invalid. The third label class is designed for
    uploading images of random objects.

9. Once all the images are uploaded, it is time to label them. Select
    the labeling queue on your dataset dashboard (Figure 6-12).

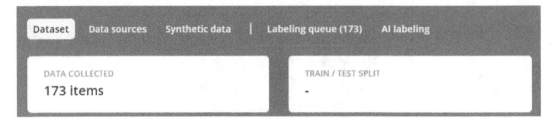

Figure 6-12. *Select labeling queue*

10. Now, drag a box around the object and create and save the label as shown in Figure 6-13. Repeat this exercise for all images in the dataset.

Figure 6-13. *Draw a box and add a label*

11. Repeat this exercise for all images in the dataset.

12. After labeling all of your images, your dataset should look something like what is shown in Figure 6-14. The images are automatically split into training and test datasets in an 80:20 ratio.

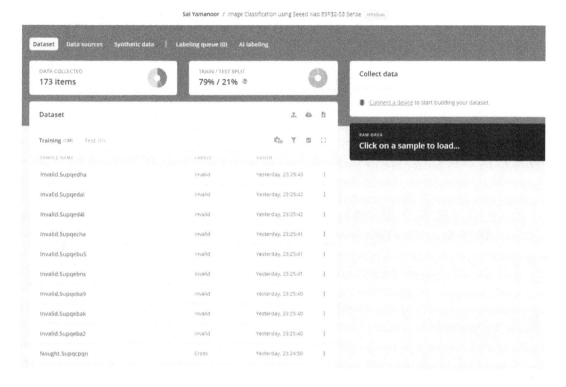

Figure 6-14. *Training and test dataset*

13. Now that we have our datasets, it is time to build an *Impulse*.
An *Impulse* refers to a pipeline where images are converted
into a format suitable for extracting the features and outputting
the features detected in the image. It essentially allows us to
define what we want to do with each image captured by the
camera sensor.

14. On the left tab of your project, click *Experiments* and then *Create a
new impulse* as shown in Figure 6-15.

Figure 6-15.   *Create a new impulse*

15.   A new *Impulse* looks something like what is shown in Figure 6-16. We need to add a processing block and a learning block.

Figure 6-16.   *New Impulse*

16.   We add a processing block for images meant to resize images and reduce the color depth (Figure 6-17).

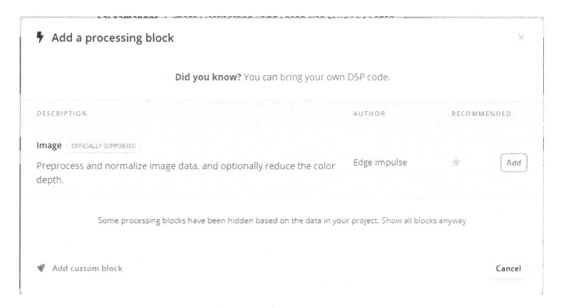

Figure 6-17. *Adding a processing block*

17. For the learning block, we add the Object Detection block
     (Figure 6-18).

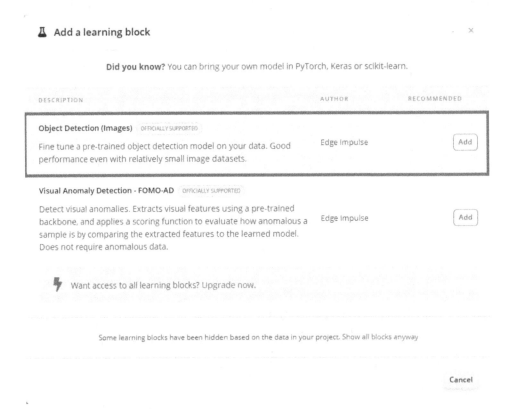

Figure 6-18. *Adding an Object Detection block*

18. Your impulse should look like what is shown in Figure 6-19. It is time to save the Impulse.

Figure 6-19. *Save Impulse*

19. Next, we need to set a new target by selecting *Target* from the top right corner (Figure 6-20).

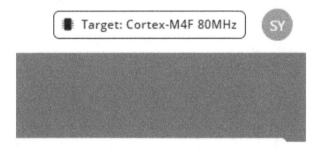

Figure 6-20. *Select Target*

20. We set the target to *ESP32* and *RAM* and *ROM* to 8 MB as shown in Figure 6-21 and save it.

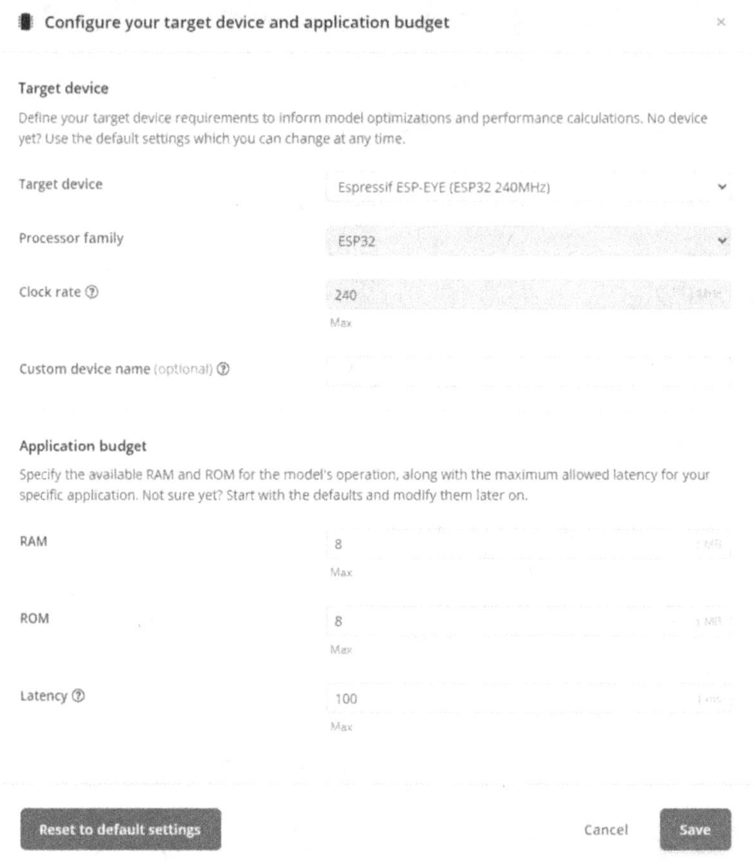

Figure 6-21. *Set target to ESP32 and save*

21. Now, it is time to generate features. From the right tab, select
     Image and select *Generate features* (Figure 6-22).

Figure 6-22. *Generate features*

22. Click Generate features as shown in Figure 6-23.

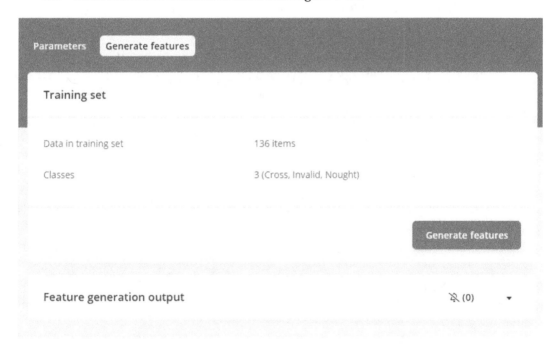

Figure 6-23. *Generate features*

23. It can take a while for the tool to finish generating features (shown in Figure 6-24).

Figure 6-24. *Generating features complete*

24. From the Object Detection tab, we will train the model on our
    dataset using the settings shown in Figure 6-25 and click *Save &*
    Train. It can take a while for the training process to complete.

Figure 6-25. *Save & Train model*

25. Once the training is completed, you will see the performance of your model including memory consumption, inference time, and RAM usage (Figure 6-26).

Figure 6-26. Training complete

26. Now, it is time to take our trained model for a spin by clicking the *Model Testing* tab from the left and clicking *Classify All*. You can now see the performance of our model as shown in Figure 6-27.

Figure 6-27. *Results from running model on test dataset*

27. It is now time to take our model for a spin on the ESP32. In the
    Deployment tab, we are presented with two options: *Quantized*
    and the *Unoptimized* model. We will make use of the *Quantized*
    model. We also selected an *Arduino library* for deployment from
    the drop-down menu at the top (as shown in Figure 6-28). Once
    the build finishes, we can download the zip file to a local folder.

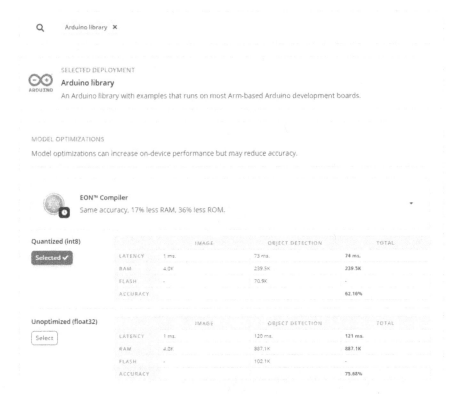

Figure 6-28. *Build an Arduino library*

28. The downloaded zip file is an Arduino library. You can add the
    library to the IDE by going to Sketch ➤ Include Library ➤ Add .ZIP
    Library and add the downloaded zip file (as shown in Figure 6-29).

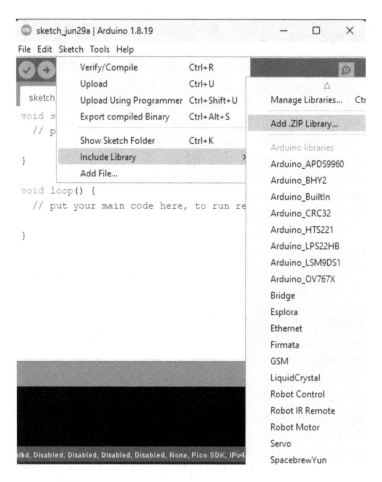

Figure 6-29. *Include Library*

29. If the library inclusion is successful, it should display the message shown in Figure 6-30.

Figure 6-30. *Library inclusion*

30. The library is now available under the examples folder of the Arduino IDE. The library name will match that of your Edge Impulse Project. Load the esp32_camera sketch as shown in Figure 6-31.

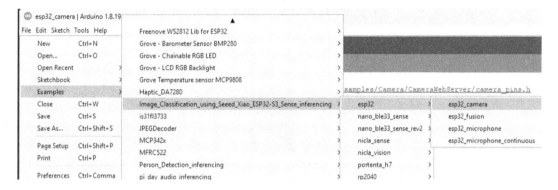

Figure 6-31. *Load the esp32_camera example*

31. The only modification needed to the sketch is that the preprocessor definition needs to be uncommented and the one on line 35 needs to be commented out.

```
//#define CAMERA_MODEL_ESP_EYE // Has PSRAM
#define CAMERA_MODEL_AI_THINKER // Has PSRAM
```

32. The ESP32-CAM module is interfaced to a USB serial adapter as shown in Figure 6-32. The pinouts are shown in Table 6-2. Apart from these connections, the pin IO0 is connected to ground at the time of flashing.

Table 6-2. *ESP32 to USB serial adapter interface*

ESP32-CAM Pin	USB Serial Adapter Pin
3.3V	3.3V
GND	GND
U0T	RX
U0R	TX

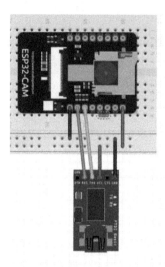

Figure 6-32. *Schematic to program ESP32-CAM using a serial adapter*

33. Now, we can compile and flash the ESP32 using the Upload button. We recommend following the instructions in Chapter 1 if you are not familiar with the Arduino IDE.

The compilation of the sketch takes a really long time because of the source files. On our workstation, it took nearly 20 minutes to compile the finish compiling!

---

34. After uploading the sketch, launch the serial terminal using the Serial Monitor button on the top right of the Arduino IDE (Figure 6-33).

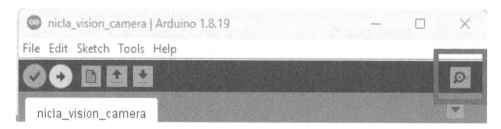

Figure 6-33. *Launch the serial monitor*

35. When you launch the serial monitor and set the baud rate to 115200 baud, you should be able to see the model performance on your ESP32. In Figure 6-34, you can see the confidence levels of each class. This is determined by capturing a frame from the camera sensor and running it through the model deployed onto the ESP32. The model deployed on the ESP32 is able to predict with 67% confidence that the object detected was a cross.

```
COM20                                                            —   □   ✕

                                                                        Send

22:28:46.473 -> Starting inferencing in 2 seconds...
22:28:48.474 -> Taking photo...
22:28:48.618 -> Predictions (DSP: 1 ms., Classification: 94 ms., Anomaly: 0 ms.):
22:28:48.618 -> Object detection bounding boxes:
22:28:48.618 ->
22:28:48.618 -> Starting inferencing in 2 seconds...
22:28:50.620 -> Taking photo...
22:28:50.763 -> Predictions (DSP: 1 ms., Classification: 94 ms., Anomaly: 0 ms.):
22:28:50.763 -> Object detection bounding boxes:
22:28:50.763 ->    Cross (0.671875) [ x: 64, y: 24, width: 8, height: 8 ]
22:28:50.763 ->
22:28:50.763 -> Starting inferencing in 2 seconds...
22:28:52.779 -> Taking photo...
22:28:52.922 -> Predictions (DSP: 1 ms., Classification: 94 ms., Anomaly: 0 ms.):
22:28:52.922 -> Object detection bounding boxes:
22:28:52.922 ->

☐ Autoscroll ☑ Show timestamp          No line ending ∨  115200 baud ∨   Clear output
```

Figure 6-34. *Serial port output of the ESP32's image classification deployment*

You will have noticed that the model performance is slightly reduced when compared to that of the Edge Impulse tool. This is because of the following reasons:

- The dataset was captured using a mobile device. Since the camera resolution is different, the model performance is affected. This can be mitigated by using the ESP32 to capture images and upload them. This resource is a useful tool to capture images (available under an Apache license) and save them to a microSD card: https://github.com/Mjrovai/XIAO-ESP32S3-Sense/tree/main/xiao_esp32s3_camera.

- Performance is generally reduced by quantization.

If we recall the TinyML product development steps from earlier, it is an iterative process. Based on the model performance, we need to repeat the data collection and model building/fine-tuning steps.

Applications for This Example

The example discussed here could be used to set up a robotic arm and play a game of tic-tac-toe. The ESP32 could be used to detect the game pieces and move them to the game board. In the real world, the ESP32 could be used to sort objects on a production line where it detects an anomaly and rejects a product. The ESP32 can play a critical role in low-power machine vision applications.

In the next section, we are going to discuss the use of the ESP32-S3 in audio-related TinyML applications.

TinyML Audio Application Example

We are going to discuss the *keyword spotting* example. *Keyword spotting* refers to detecting the utterance of a word in an audio sample. A significant application of keyword spotting is voice assistants on smartphones. Keyword spotting works by looking at audio signatures collected from an audio sample. You can read more about keyword spotting here: `https://www.tensorflow.org/tutorials/audio/simple_audio`.

Applications similar to keyword spotting include

- Predictive maintenance of components like bearings in industrial machinery by detecting strange sounds from the equipment

- Detection of anomalies or leaks in the system by listening for strange sounds in a pressure manifold

- Detection of poaching activity by listening for buzzsaw sounds

According to Espressif, the example discussed in this section should work with ESP32, ESP32-S3, ESP32-P4, and ESP32-C3 microcontrollers. You should be able to migrate your application with relative ease within the Espressif family.

Schematic

For this example, we need the SPH0645LM4H I²S Microphone Breakout (price: 6.95 USD) from Adafruit. It is available here: `https://www.adafruit.com/product/3421`. The microphone is interfaced to the Adafruit Metro ESP32-S3 (Figure 6-35) as shown in Table 6-3.

Table 6-3. *Adafruit Metro ESP32-S3 to SPH0645LM4H interface*

Adafruit Metro ESP32-S3 Pinout	SPH0645LM4H Pinout
3.3V	3.3V
GND	GND
MOSI (GPIO 42)	BCLK
RX (GPIO 41)	DOUT
SEL	GND
LRCL	GND

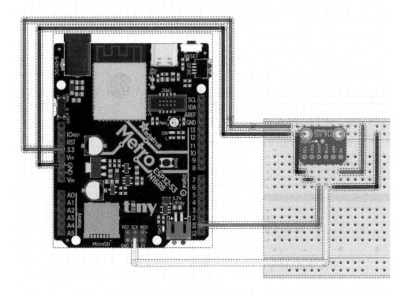

Figure 6-35. *Adafruit Metro ESP32-S3 – I²S Microphone schematic*

Code Sample Modification

The example discussed in this section is based on the `micro_speech` example available here: `https://github.com/espressif/esp-tflite-micro/tree/master/examples/micro_speech`. It is available under an Apache license. The modified code sample is available for download along with this chapter.

Description of the Example

The micro speech example is designed to detect three states:

- **Keyword *yes* detected:** In this case, the audio signature for the word yes was detected.

- **Keyword *no* detected:** The audio signature for the word no was detected.

- ***Unknown* keyword detected:** The audio sample was silent or some unknown keyword was detected.

Prerequisite Installation

For this example, the ESP-IDF framework is required. Espressif provides detailed instructions on how to install the framework. The instructions are available here: `https://github.com/espressif/vscode-esp-idf-extension/blob/master/README.md`.

- Once the instructions are installed in VS Code, open a folder on your desktop and launch the ESP-IDF framework as shown in Figure 6-36.

Figure 6-36. *Launch the ESP-IDF framework*

Launch the ESP-IDF terminal as shown in Figure 6-37.

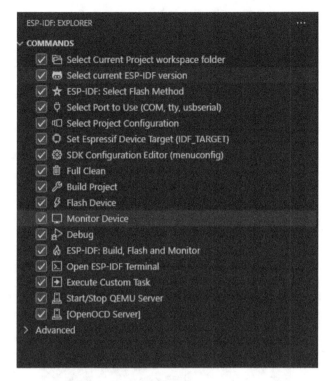

Figure 6-37. *Launch the ESP-IDF terminal*

From the ESP-IDF terminal, run the following commands:

```
idf.py add-dependency "esp-tflite-micro"
idf.py create-project-from-example "esp-tflite-micro:micro_speech
```

The ESP-IDF terminal can be launched from the ESP-IDF Explorer Extension as shown in Figure 6-38.

Figure 6-38. *Launch the ESP-IDF terminal*

This would create the *micro_speech* example in your local directory (Figure 6-39).

Figure 6-39. *micro_speech code sample created in the local directory*

We need to modify the code sample to set the connections to the microphone breakout board. The following preprocessor macro is added to line 42:

```
#define CONFIG_IDF_TARGET_ESP32S3 1
```

The code between lines 97 and 101 are modified as follows:

```
i2s_pin_config_t pin_config = {
     .bck_io_num = 42,
     .ws_io_num = -1,
     .data_out_num = -1,
     .data_in_num = 41,
  };
```

After saving the modifications to the file, the target is set to ESP32-S3 as follows from the ESP-IDF terminal (shown earlier in the code):

```
idf.py set-target esp32s3
```

We build the project with the following command:

```
idf.py build
```

The build takes a while to compile for the first time. The binary could be flashed onto the Adafruit ESP32-S3. If you have MicroPython flashed onto the board, you will have to set the board to bootloader mode. If you don't know the serial port for your board, follow the instructions from Chapter 1.

```
idf.py --port COM34 flash
```

Now, we can take a live look at the ESP32-S3 microcontroller, capturing live audio from the I²S interface and running the keyword detection model.

```
idf.py --port COM34 monitor
```

The program running on the ESP32-S3 outputs something like what is shown in Figure 6-40.

```
I (251) heap_init: At 600FE11C len 0001ECC (7 KiB): RTCRAM
I (257) spi_flash: detected chip: gd
I (259) spi_flash: flash io: qio
W (262) spi_flash: Detected size(8192k) larger than the size in the binary image header(2048k). Using the size in the binary image header.
W (275) i2s(legacy): legacy i2s driver is deprecated, please migrate to use driver/i2s_std.h, driver/i2s_pdm.h or driver/i2s_tdm.h
I (286) sleep_gpio: Configure to isolate all GPIO pins in sleep state
I (292) sleep_gpio: Enable automatic switching of GPIO sleep configuration
I (299) main_task: Started on CPU0
I (309) main_task: Calling app_main()
I (329) feature_provider: InitializeMicroFeatures successful
I (389) TF_LITE_AUDIO_PROVIDER: Audio Recording started
Detected      yes, score: 0.61
Detected      yes, score: 0.44
Detected unknown, score: 0.73
Detected unknown, score: 0.47
Detected unknown, score: 0.81
Detected      yes, score: 0.73
Detected unknown, score: 0.66
```

Figure 6-40. *micro_speech example output*

Try uttering *yes* and *no* to check for the keywords detected by the model running on the microcontroller. This example prints out any keyword for which the confidence score exceeds 80% (0.8). If no keyword is detected (*Detected unknown*), line 169 in *main_functions.cc* needs to be modified where the confidence level is set to a lower threshold.

```
if (max_result > 0.4f) {
    MicroPrintf("Detected %7s, score: %.2f", kCategoryLabels[max_idx],
        static_cast<double>(max_result));
}
```

When we ran this example, we had to lower the threshold to 40% (0.4). This could be attributed to the microphone performance. After adjusting the threshold, the example must be re-compiled and tested.

Now that we have tested a TinyML application, we will discuss some challenges with taking TinyML products to the market.

TinyML Product Development Challenges

There are some considerations to keep in mind before you take your product to the market.

- **Product volume considerations:** TinyML is suitable for applications where the product is expected to have a large fleet. This helps avoid creating data lakes due to the large fleet. The effort to develop a TinyML-enabled product is not worth it for a one-off low-volume product.

- **Data characterization:** It is important to understand the overall characteristics of the data generated by the product's sensors, including any edge cases observed in the field. This is only possible by deploying a small fleet in different scenarios and collecting data.

- **Application suitability:** Before investing a lot of time into building a machine learning model for your application, it is crucial to determine whether it is possible to discern distinct events by looking at the data. If so, a machine learning model can make that inference. We recommended that machine learning models be used in safety engineering-related applications with caution.

- **Performance fine-tuning:** Your model needs extensive fine-tuning based on data collected over time. This means that the product must be designed to perform over-the-air firmware updates.

- **Model selection:** Since machine learning involves running a model tested and tuned to run in the cloud, selecting the right model for your application is critical. There is some drop in performance when the model is converted to run on a microcontroller.

- **Traceability:** Your product must be designed to capture all data around an inference event. This includes a timestamp, the raw data behind the inference, etc. This helps weed out any false positives. A lot of data collection and fine-tuning is required to improve performance.

Conclusion

In this chapter, we discussed the concept of developing TinyML-enabled IoT products, the need for TinyML, and its importance in IoT applications. We picked an image classification example for ESP32-CAM and a keyword detection example and customized it for the Adafruit Metro ESP32-S3. We also discussed the challenges behind developing TinyML-enabled products. In the next chapter, we will use the tools we have learned so far to build a full-fledged wearable product!

CHAPTER 7

Let's Build a Product!

We have reviewed the various features of the ESP32 microcontroller and its applications. In this chapter, we will work on building a prototype for an ESP32 microcontroller-enabled IoT product. By the end of this chapter, you should be able to create a prototype like the one shown in Figure 7-1.

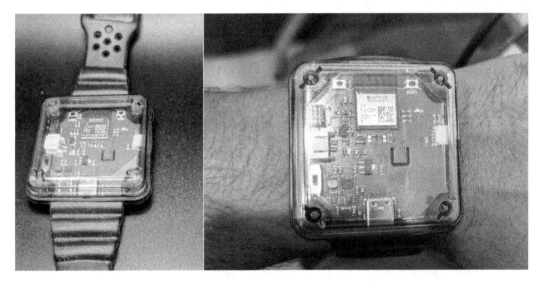

Figure 7-1. *Wearable prototype*

The wearable prototype shown in the previous picture uses an ESP32-C6-MINI-1 module. We will discuss why we chose to replace the ESP32-S3 we chose in Chapter 1. This is due to the lack of components available while building the prototype.

© Sai Yamanoor and Srihari Yamanoor 2025
S. Yamanoor and S. Yamanoor, *IoT Product Development Using ESP32 Microcontrollers*,
https://doi.org/10.1007/979-8-8688-1570-6_7

Components Required

We are building a prototype for our product, so some investment is required. You also need PCB (printed circuit board) design software. We recommend using KiCad (`https://www.kicad.org/`), an open source design software. If you are unfamiliar with PCB design, plenty of tutorials are available, but we recommend this one from KiCad: `https://docs.kicad.org/9.0/en/getting_started_in_kicad/getting_started_in_kicad.html`. You might need some components for breadboarding a prototype.

In this chapter, we built our prototype using Autodesk Eagle. You should be able to import our design files into KiCad and use it. We used Eagle for our convenience, as the design process is similar across tools.

Capturing Product Requirements

Let's assume we are building a non-clinical personal health monitoring wearable for our customers. Let's also discuss a few other requirements from the customer:

1. The customer wants to monitor their heart rate, blood oxygen levels, and skin temperature.

2. The customer wants to be able to transmit the collected sensor data to a mobile device or another ESP32-based Bluetooth gateway.

3. The customer wants a prototype to prove the wearable concept. They want the form factor to be something that could be worn around the wrist or as a pendant around the neck.

4. To prove the concept, the customer does not want a display for the wearable.

5. The customer wants to determine the technical feasibility before working out the details, such as enclosure selection, fit, etc.

We can assume that the customer will use this device only in a non-clinical setting, and this wearable will not be used as a medical device.

Breadboarding a Prototype

This chapter's example closely follows the Bluetooth examples in Chapter 4. We recommend following that chapter to build prototypes for your sensors. We will discuss the electrical connections and the code samples for the sensors selected through various chapter sections.

Sensor Selection

The sensors we chose for our prototype are equipped with an I²C interface. We will discuss the selected sensors.

MAX30102

The MAX30102 is an integrated pulse oximetry and heart-rate sensor equipped with an I²C interface. A prototyping breakout board for this sensor can be purchased here: `https://www.digikey.com/en/products/detail/dfrobot/SEN0518/18069209`.

TMP117

This is a medical-grade, high-precision digital temperature sensor equipped with an I²C interface. A breakout board for this sensor can be purchased here: `https://www.sparkfun.com/sparkfun-high-precision-temperature-sensor-tmp117-qwiic.html`.

The first step is to wire the sensors and get them working before building our proof of concept. At this point, we can communicate with the sensor and get some data from it. For now, we can assume that we got the sensor working and move on to the next step, where we draw the schematic for our prototype.

Schematic Capture

Schematic capture is the process by which we create a schematic for our design. This step involves selecting the components required for our design, creating schematic symbols, and drawing up the electrical connections required for our design. Schematic capture in PCB design is the equivalent of drawing up a blueprint for a building before starting construction.

Let's review the various components we are going to wire up in this schematic and the reason for their selection. The schematic discussed in this section is available for download along with this chapter.

In order to create schematics, we used the schematic symbols and footprints available from SnapEDA (https://www.snapeda.com/). The schematic and footprints are available under a CC-BY-SA license. SnapEDA permits the use of schematic symbols and footprints in commercial designs without attribution. Next, we will discuss some key components related to the ESP32 module.

ESP32-Module Selection

In this book, we have been discussing the use of ESP32-S3 modules, and we must use an ESP32-S3 module in our design. Unfortunately, the vendor that we used for fabricating the boards didn't have any suitable ESP32-S3 modules in stock. So we opted to use the ESP32-C6 module for our design. This shouldn't be a problem, as any code written in MicroPython for the ESP32-S3 module can be ported to the ESP32-C6. The only changes required might be the pins used when we switch out the modules. Figure 7-2 shows the schematic for the ESP32-C6 module. This schematic was prepared in accordance with the manufacturer guidelines available here: https://docs.espressif.com/projects/esp-hardware-design-guidelines/en/latest/esp32c6/schematic-checklist.html. The module is powered by a 3.3V source.

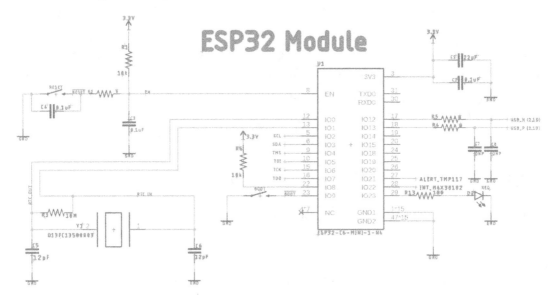

Figure 7-2. *ESP32-C6 module schematic*

Filtering and Decoupling capacitors

The manufacturer recommends adding two filter capacitors with values of 22μF and 0.1μF (as shown in Figure 7-3). These capacitors must be placed closer to the power pin of the module. These capacitors act as reservoirs, helping to smooth out any fluctuations in voltage and prevent resets of the module due to under-voltage issues.

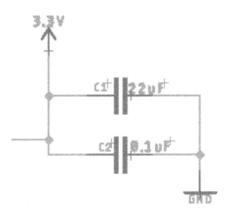

Figure 7-3. *Filter capacitors*

Reset Circuit

The reset pin is an active-low pin, i.e., the module resets itself when connected to the ground for at least 50 microseconds (according to the datasheet). The reset pin should always be pulled up with a weak resistor to 3.3V. The manufacturer recommends adding an RC circuit with a 10 kilo-ohms pull-up resistor and a 1.0μF capacitor for the reset circuit (as shown in Figure 7-4). We also added a tactile switch where one end connects to the EN pin while the other connects to the ground. A 0.1μF capacitor across the button acts as a debounce circuit, preventing noise-related false triggers.

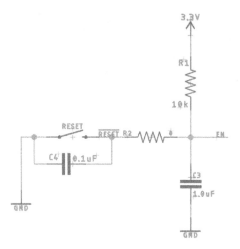

Figure 7-4. *Reset circuit*

Bootstrapping Pins

According to the datasheet, GPIO pins 8 and 9 are considered *bootstrapping* pins. They control the ESP32-C6 microcontroller's bootloader mode. After reset, the microcontroller enters the bootloader mode if GPIO pin 8 is high and GPIO 9 is low. This enables us to load the MicroPython binary onto the microcontroller. So we pull up GPIO pin 8 to 3.3V using a 10 kilo-ohm resistor and add a *BOOT* button to GPIO pin 9. The other end of the button is connected to the ground. As discussed in Chapter 1, the bootloader mode can be initiated by pressing the reset button once while simultaneously holding the boot button. Figure 7-5 shows the bootstrapping circuit.

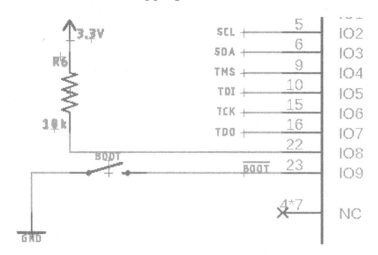

Figure 7-5. *Bootstrapping, debugging, and I²C circuit*

I²C Circuit

As discussed in Chapter 3, I²C communications require a *Clock* (SCL) and a *Data* (SDA) pin. Figure 7-5 shows that we assigned GPIO pins 2 and 3 for the I²C interface. We also need to pull up resistors for the clock and data pins. We will discuss this in the MAX30102 Sensor section.

Debugging Circuitry

We added a JTAG debug interface (as shown in Figure 7-6) for our customers to debug their application code. When the JTAG debugger is connected to the microcontroller, it is possible to track variables and add breakpoints to the code for debugging. We also added a standard JTAG connector to connect the debugging cable to the board.

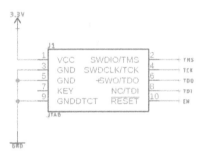

Figure 7-6. *JTAG debugging circuit*

USB Interface

GPIO pins 12 and 13 can be used as a USB Serial interface, enabling the download of code onto the microcontroller. The hardware design guidelines also recommend adding a zero-ohm resistor closer to the module and a reserve footprint for a capacitor. We will discuss the USB connector details in a later section. The nets *USB_N* and *USB_P* in Figure 7-7 refer to the pins of the USB interface.

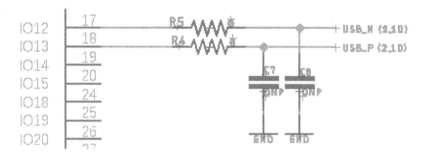

Figure 7-7. *USB interface*

Debug LED

We added an LED for debugging purposes. We will use this LED after flashing the MicroPython binary to determine whether everything is working as expected. The LED can also be used for fault indication or to signal special events detected by the firmware. Figure 7-8 shows the schematic for the LED with a 100 ohm resistor in series.

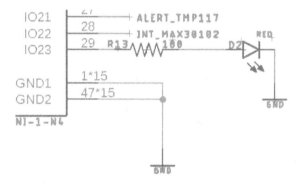

Figure 7-8. *Debug LED and interrupt pins*

Interrupt Pins

Figure 7-8 also shows two nets apart from the LED, namely, ALERT_TMP117 and INT_MAX30102. They are meant for interrupts generated by the temperature and heart rate sensors. An interrupt is a special alert generated by a sensor. The alert can be configured for scenarios such as temperature exceeding the limit or when a new sensor reading is available.

Real-Time Clock

We added a 32.768 kHz real-time clock crystal (shown in Figure 7-9) for timekeeping purposes while our wearable is in the deep sleep state. The clock is connected to GPIO pins 0 and 1. A 1 megaohm resistor is added in parallel to the crystal. Two load capacitors are added per the crystal's requirements.

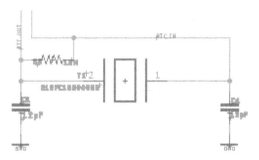

Figure 7-9. *External real-time clock crystal*

TMP117 Sensor

The TMP117 sensor is equipped with an I²C interface. The sensor's clock and data pins are connected to the ESP32-C6 module using the nets SCL and SDA, respectively. The TMP117 pin has an *ALERT* pin, which generates an interrupt when configured. The *ALERT* pin is connected to the module using the *ALERT_TMP117* net. The interrupt pin is open-drain, i.e., interrupts are generated by pulling the pin low. So the pin is pulled up to 3.3V using a 10 kilo-ohm resistor. The pin *ADD0* can be used to set the sensor's address. It is tied to the ground to set the address to 0x48. It is possible to set a different address if you have more than one TMP117 sensor on the I²C bus. You can read about the address configuration in the datasheet (available here: https://www.ti.com/lit/ds/symlink/tmp117.pdf). A 0.1µF decoupling capacitor is added to the sensor to smooth out any voltage ripples. This capacitor must be placed as close to the sensor as possible. The sensor is powered by a 3.3V source. The TMP117 Sensor schematic is shown in Figure 7-10.

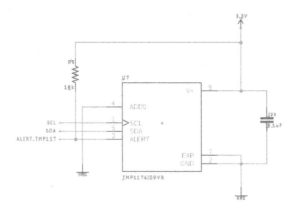

Figure 7-10. *TMP117 sensor*

MAX30102 Sensor

The connections for the MAX30102 sensor (shown in Figure 7-11) are similar to those of the TMP117 sensor, where the clock and data pins are connected to the ESP32 with the CLOCK and DATA nets, respectively. The interrupt pin INT is connected to ESP32 through the INT_MAX30102 net. A pull-up resistor is used since it is an open-drain output. We also add pull-up resistors to the SCL and SDA nets (explanation provided in Chapter 3). The sensor requires two power supplies: 3.3V and 1.1V. We also added filter capacitors as recommended by the manufacturer.

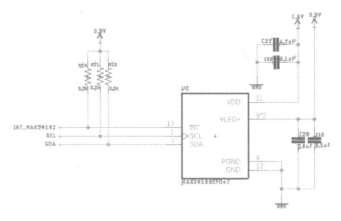

Figure 7-11. *MAX30102 schematic*

Qwiic Sensor Interface

We added a four-pin connector, known as the Qwiic Sensor Connector, to our design. This enables our customers to further this prototype by adding an external sensor. The part number for this connector is *SM04B-SRSS-TB(LF)(SN)*. We did a deeper dive on the pin connections in Chapter 3. The connector must be wired in the order shown in Figure 7-12.

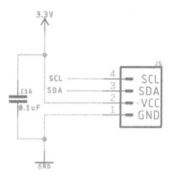

Figure 7-12. *Qwiic Sensor Port schematic*

Putting it all together, the first page of our schematic resembles the one shown in Figure 7-13.

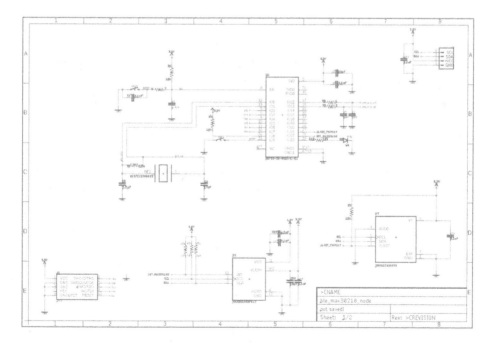

Figure 7-13. *Page 1 of schematic*

Power Circuitry

Our design can be powered via USB or an external battery. We will discuss the power elements of the schematic.

Battery Connector and Switch

Figure 7-14 shows the battery connection schematic. We also added a double-pole, double-throw switch to disconnect the battery.

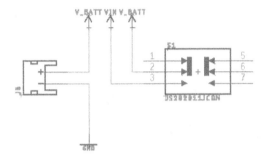

Figure 7-14. *Battery connector schematic*

USB Connector and Ideal Diodes

We added a USB-C connector to the design and 5.1 kilo-ohm resistors to the CC1 and CC2 pins. This limits the current draw to 500 mA, which is more than sufficient for our design. The USB bus power net includes a pi filter for removing high-frequency noise. The filter consists of two 0.1µF capacitors and a 2.2 nH inductor.

The USB power source (*V_USB_IN*) and the battery power source (*VIN*) are connected to the buck-boost regulator through ideal diodes. The diodes prevent reverse current flow when both sources are turned on. When the wearable is powered via USB, the ideal diode allows current to flow from *V_USB_IN*. When the USB power source is disconnected, the input power source automatically switches over to the buck-boost regulator.

The part number of the ideal diode used in this design is *LM66100DCKR*. Figure 7-15 shows the schematic for the USB connector and the diode configuration used in this design.

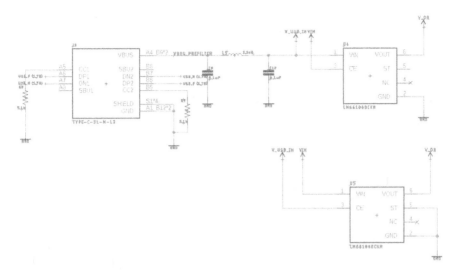

Figure 7-15. *USB connector schematic*

Battery Charging Circuit

Figure 7-16 illustrates the battery charging circuit for the wearable device. We used the MCP73831 Lithium Battery Charge Management Controller. The charging current is limited to 500 mA with the 2 kilo-ohm resistor added to the *PROG* pin. A red LED is added to the STAT pin of the charger, providing an indication when the battery charging is complete. The battery is charged using the USB power source.

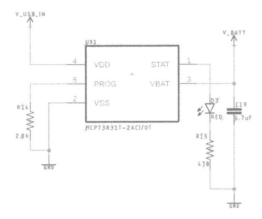

Figure 7-16. *Battery charging circuit*

Buck-Boost Regulator

We chose the TPS63001 buck-boost converter for this design because it has a 3.3V output and is suitable for battery-powered designs. We adopted the circuit shown in Figure 7-17 from the application note provided in the datasheet (available here: https://www.ti.com/lit/ds/symlink/tps63001.pdf).

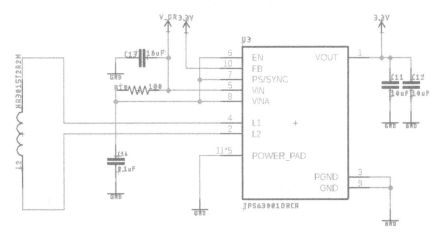

Figure 7-17. *Buck-boost circuit*

1.8V Low-Dropout Regulator

We need a 1.8V power supply for the MAX30102 heart rate sensor, so we added a 1.8V low-dropout (LDO) regulator (as shown in Figure 7-18). The regulator's input power supply is 3.3V from the buck-boost converter. We also added a filter capacitor to the regulator's input and output.

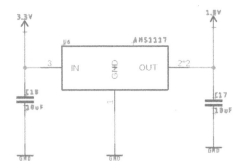

Figure 7-18. *LDO circuit*

Putting it all together, the entire power supply circuitry schematic looks like the one shown in Figure 7-19.

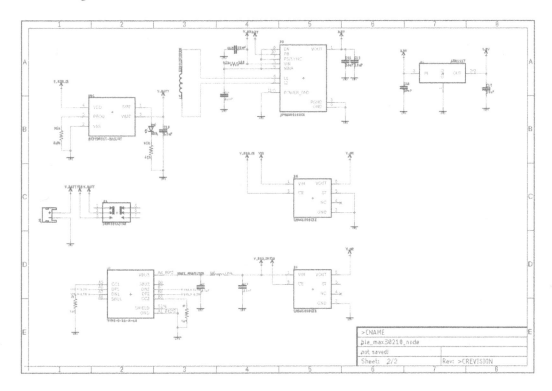

Figure 7-19. *Power supply schematic*

Electrical Rule Check

After completing the schematic, PCB software tools offer a rule-checking tool that helps check the schematic for any gross violations in our schematic. We reviewed and fixed all warnings and errors after running an electrical rule check (as shown in Figure 7-20).

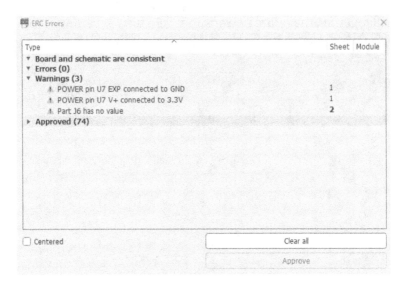

Figure 7-20. *Electrical rule check output*

Now that the schematic capture is complete, we move on to the PCB layout process.

PCB Layout

In this section, we are going to discuss the layout process for the PCB.

Enclosure Selection

The first step is selecting an enclosure for our wearable. After some web search, we landed on a wearable enclosure from Serpac: `https://www.serpac.com/waterproof-wrist-enclosures-bw4.html`. We chose this enclosure because

1. The enclosure form factor is suitable for wearing as a wristwatch and a pendant. The manufacturer supplies pendant enclosures as a variant for this wearable enclosure.

2. The manufacturer provides the step files for the enclosure and the recommended board layout.

3. The unit cost of the enclosure is around 5.30 USD.

This enclosure is a great place to start for our design.

Board Shape Import

We downloaded the step files needed for our design and generated a board outline suitable for Autodesk Eagle. This step might vary for other PCB design software tools. A board outline for our wearable design is shown in Figure 7-21. The board outline is available for download directly from the manufacturer's website.

Figure 7-21. *Wearable board outline file*

Component Placement and Layout

Autodesk Eagle offers options to import board outlines from Fusion 360. After importing the outline, we place the components in the board area. We placed all the elements discussed in the schematic capture section onto the board. All components except for the sensors are placed on the top side. The sensors are placed on the bottom side because they could be used for heart rate and temperature measurements through an aperture in the enclosure. The sensors are placed on the board according to the manufacturer's recommendations. The temperature sensor is placed with a milled slot. This is to avoid the sensor being affected by any heat source on the board. We also ensured that the component placement did not interfere with the walls of the enclosure.

1. The ESP32-C6 module is placed on one end of the board as recommended by Espressif.

2. The USB-C connector is placed on the opposite side of the ESP32 module.

3. The battery connector, switch, and the Qwiic I²C connector are placed outward on the board's remaining two sides.

4. We also ensure that all components are placed at least 0.030 inches away from the edges to avoid the PCB clamping area inside the enclosure.

Once the component placement is finalized, deciding on the board stack-up is the next step.

Board Stack-up

A board stack-up refers to how the signals and the voltages will be routed on the board. Depending on the design complexity, a board can have 1, 2, 4, 6, 8, or 16 layers. Espressif recommends designing a four-layer stack-up for their modules. If you are on a tight budget, a two-layer stack-up should also be sufficient. Here is how we adopted the four-layer stack-up:

1. **Top layer – signal layer:** All signals need to be routed in this layer, with some exceptions.

2. **Ground layer:** Provides the path for the return current for all components.

3. **Power supply layer:** All signals from the power supplies to the individual components are routed through this layer.

4. **Bottom layer:** Any signal that cannot be routed through the top layer are routed through this layer using a via.

Now that the board stack-up is decided, we will route the board and perform a design rule check.

Board Layout

We are ready to route the traces between the components in this stage. We determine the trace width depending on the nature of the signal. For example, we ensure that all traces are at least 10 mils wide and all vias are at least 15 mils in diameter. We ensure that power supply traces' width is determined according to their peak current requirements.

After we finish routing the board, it is time to perform a *design rule check*. These checks are performed according to the rules and specifications provided by the manufacturer we will use for fabrication. Some board houses provide a design rule file for popular PCB design software tools. Here are some examples of design rule files available from PCB manufacturers:

1. OSH Park: `https://github.com/OSHPark/OSHPark-Eagle-Tools`

2. JLCPCB: `https://jlcpcb.com/blog/how-to-run-a-design-rule-check-for-your-pcbs`

We fixed any violation pointed out by the design rule check tool. Figure 7-22 shows the output of the design rule check.

Figure 7-22. *Design rule check*

In Autodesk Eagle, the completed design file looks something like the image shown in Figure 7-23.

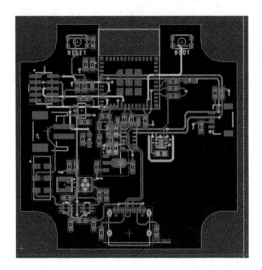

Figure 7-23. *Completed board layout*

Component Placement Verification

Once the layout and design rule check are completed, we associate the 3D models of the components of our board and push them to the board's 3D model. We share the 3D model with the customer to ensure their satisfaction with the placement. Figure 7-24 shows the top and bottom views of the board's 3D model.

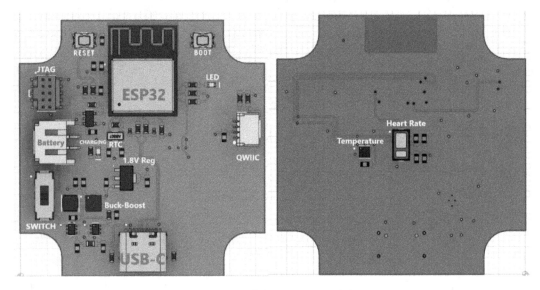

Figure 7-24. *Top and bottom views of the PCB model*

We also ensure that the board fits inside the enclosure without any interference with the walls of the enclosure. Figure 7-25 shows the fit of the board inside the enclosure.

Figure 7-25. *Board fit inside the enclosure*

We also perform a cross section to ensure the components fit inside the enclosure on both sides. Figure 7-26 shows a cross section of the wearable.

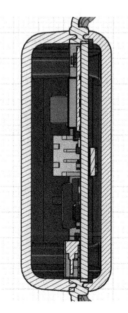

Figure 7-26. *Cross section of the wearable*

Gerber File Generation

Once we have finished verifying that the components have been placed and routed carefully, we can generate the Gerber files for manufacturing. Gerber files provide detailed instructions to the manufacturer for fabricating the board. This includes any drill instructions, signal/copper traces in all layers, milling instructions, etc. Since we will be using JLCPCB for fabricating the boards, we will be using the CAM file provided by them to generate the Gerber files. Figure 7-27 shows a snapshot of the Gerber files generated using the CAM file.

ble_max30210_node_copper_I1.GTL	GTL File
ble_max30210_node_copper_I2.G1	G1 File
ble_max30210_node_copper_I3.G2	G2 File
ble_max30210_node_copper_I4.GBL	GBL File
ble_max30210_node_drill.XLN	XLN File
ble_max30210_node_Legend_Bot.GBO	GBO File
ble_max30210_node_Legend_Top.GTO	GTO File
ble_max30210_node_Paste_Bot.GBP	GBP File
ble_max30210_node_Paste_Top.GTP	GTP File
ble_max30210_node_Profile_NP.GKO	GKO File
ble_max30210_node_Soldermask_Bot.GBS	GBS File
ble_max30210_node_Soldermask_Top.GTS	GTS File

Figure 7-27. *Gerber files generated using the CAM file*

Bill of Materials

The next step is to create a Bill of Materials for the board manufacturer. Figure 7-28 lists the components of the wearable, their reference designations, footprints, and their part numbers. This is a crucial step because it is the designer's responsibility to source components and ensure that they are in stock. The part number in the last column corresponds to the part number on the board manufacturer's parts sourcing website.

Comment	Designator	Footprint	JLCPCB Part #
0	R2 R4 R5	0603	C130238
0.1uF	C2 C3 C4 C9 C10 C14 C16 C15 C22 C23	0603	C80516
2.0k	R14	0603	C269690
2.2k	R11 R12 R16	0603	C114662
2.2nH	L1	0603	C317980
4.7uF	C19 C21	0603	C99229
5.1k	R7 R8	0603	C318133
10M	R3	0603	C114606
10k	R1 R6 R9	0603	C2087321
10uF	C11 C12 C13 C17 C18 C20	0603	C91150
12pF	C5 C6	0603	C1642
22uF	C1	0603	C109448
100	R10 R13	0603	C245184
470	R15	0603	C881392
AMS1117	U6	SOT150P410X160-3N	C24247
DNP	C7 C8	0402	DNP
ESP32-C6-MINI-1-N4	U1	XCVR_ESP32-C6-MINI-1-N4	C5736265
JS202011JCQN	S1	SW_JS202011JCQN	C221665
JTAG	J1	2X5-SMD-UNSHROUDED	C448647
LM66100DCKR	U4 U5	SOT65P210X110-6N	C2869734
MCP73831T-2ACI/OT	U$1	SOT95P280X145-5N	C424093
MOMENTARY-SWITCH-SPST-	BOOT RESET	TACTILE_SWITCH_SMD_4.6X2.8MM	C72443
NR3015T2R2M	L2	IND_NR3015T2R2M	C86423
Q13FC13500003	Y1	XTAL_FC-135_32.7680KA-A0	C99010
RED	D2 D3	LED-0603	C2286
TPS63001DRCR	U3	VREG_V62/16624-01YE	C28060
TYPE-C-31-M-12	J2	HRO_TYPE-C-31-M-12	C165948
MAX30102EFD+T	U2	XDCR_MAX30101EFD+	C6454833
TMP117AIDRVR	U7	SON65P200X200X80-7N	C699536
Qwiic	J5	1mm	C160404
LiPo	J6	JST PH-2	C295747

Figure 7-28. *Bill of Materials for wearable*

Pick and Place File

Next, we generate the pick and place file containing all components' centroid data. This data is required by the manufacturer for automated assembly of the boards. Figure 7-29 shows a sample of the pick-and-place data generated for the wearable.

Designator	Mid X	Mid Y	Layer	Rotation
BOOT	34.93	43.18	Top	180
C1	13.97	38.48	Top	90
C2	15.49	38.48	Top	90
C3	15.37	34.04	Top	270
C4	15.6	43.1	Top	90
C5	16.89	22.61	Top	270
C6	19.43	22.61	Top	270
C7	25.53	26.54	Top	90
C8	20.96	26.54	Top	90
C9	15.7	5.05	Top	90
C10	10.69	5.05	Top	90
C11	11.94	17.14	Top	90
C12	10.41	17.14	Top	90
C13	9.91	10.67	Top	0
C14	18.41	11.18	Top	90
C16	38.99	25.4	Top	90
C17	24.21	17.07	Top	270
C18	16.36	17.12	Top	90
C19	13.74	26.42	Top	0
D2	36.6	35.03	Top	0
D3	14.78	22.89	Top	270
J1	4.95	33.53	Top	270
J2	23.42	3.3	Top	0
J5	41.27	26.92	Top	90
J6	5.59	24.51	Top	90

Figure 7-29. *Pick-and-place data*

Quote Generation

We are ready to get the boards manufactured by JLCPCB. We upload the Gerber, BoM, and pick-and-place files to their website and generate a quote. If you are not familiar with the process, we recommend following their tutorials to generate a quote. The quote generated by the manufacturer for fabricating five boards costs 130 USD. The manufacturer reviews the submitted files upon receiving the payment. The manufacturer reviews the design files for manufacturability and sends a snapshot of component placement. Figure 7-30 shows the component placement provided by the manufacturer.

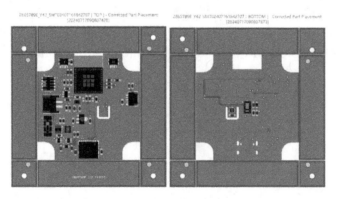

Figure 7-30. *Component placement review provided by the manufacturer*

Assembly Confirmation

The manufacturer sends a picture of the assembled boards to confirm whether all placements are correct. This is the last opportunity to catch any problems before the boards are shipped. Figure 7-31 shows the pictures shared by the manufacturer.

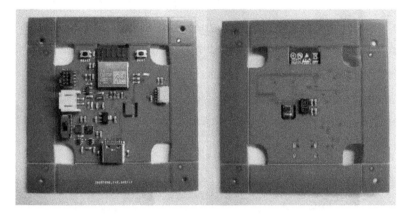

Figure 7-31. *Assembled boards shared by the manufacturer*

Board Bring-Up

The boards typically arrive somewhere between two to three weeks after the order is placed. Once the board arrives, we need to perform the board bring-up. Board bring-up is a process where we test every aspect of the board. We will cover them here.

1. The first step is to break the board rails shown in Figure 7-32. Needle-nose pliers should be sufficient to break them free.

Figure 7-32. *Breaking the rails with pliers*

2. Once the board rails have been removed, the next step is to use a multimeter to check for electrical shorts.

3. The next step is to download the MicroPython binary for the ESP32-C6 module. The binary can be downloaded from here: `https://micropython.org/download/ESP32_GENERIC_C6/`.

4. We connect the board to a computer using a USB-C cable. We set it in bootloader mode by pressing the *RESET* button once while the *BOOT* button is pressed.

5. Using instructions from Chapter 1, we flash the binary onto the module. The only difference in this step is that we set the module to be ESP32-C6, as shown in Figure 7-33.

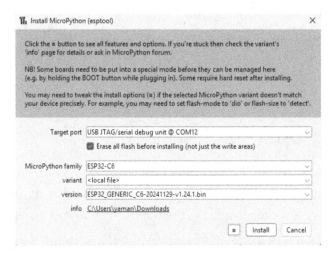

Figure 7-33. *Flashing the MicroPython binary onto the ESP32-C6 module*

6. After flashing the binary and resetting the module, the MicroPython interpreter shows up, as shown in Figure 7-34.

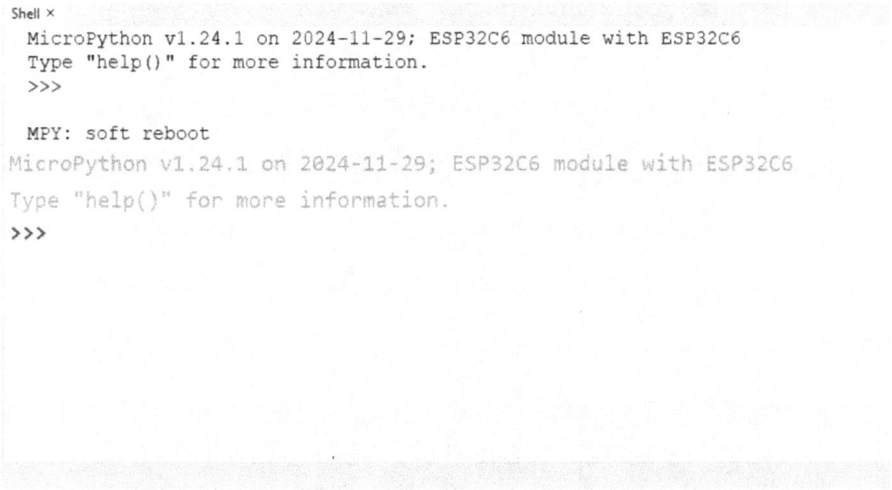

```
Shell ×
  MicroPython v1.24.1 on 2024-11-29; ESP32C6 module with ESP32C6
  Type "help()" for more information.
  >>>

  MPY: soft reboot
  MicroPython v1.24.1 on 2024-11-29; ESP32C6 module with ESP32C6
  Type "help()" for more information.
  >>>
```

Figure 7-34. *MicroPython interpreter running on the ESP32-C6 module*

7. Let's take it for a spin by making the LED connected to GPIO pin
    23 at a one-second interval. Paste the following code into the
    editor and save it as main.py on the ESP32-C6 module.

```python
from time import sleep
from machine import Pin

led = Pin(23, Pin.OUT)

while True:
    led.value(1)
    sleep(1)
    led.value(0)
    sleep(1)
```

8. Upon hitting the Run button in the Thonny IDE, the LED
    should start blinking, as shown in Figure 7-35. We also use this
    as an opportunity to test the battery circuitry by connecting a
    rechargeable LiPo battery to the connector. Since we are able to
    blink an LED, we know that the LED works.

Figure 7-35. *LED blinking test*

9. Let's ensure that the sensors are working by scanning for them on the I²C bus. To perform a scan, we need to run the following code:

```
from machine import SoftI2C

i2c = SoftI2C(scl=2, sda=3, freq=400000)
results = [hex(address) for address in i2c.scan()]
print("The devices on the I2C bus are:", *results)
```

10. We get an output similar to that shown in Figure 7-36. The I²C bus scan detected the TMP117 sensor at 0x48 and the MAX30102 sensor at 0x57.

```
Shell ×
>>> %Run -c $EDITOR_CONTENT

  MPY: soft reboot
  The devices on the I2C bus are: 0x48 0x57

>>>
```

Figure 7-36. *I²C bus scan output*

11. When we connect the battery and the USB cable to the board, the
battery should start charging. After the battery is fully charged, the
battery status LED turns on as shown in Figure 7-37.

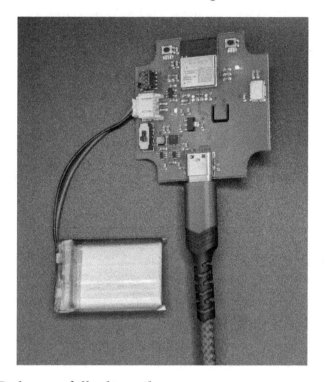

Figure 7-37. *LiPo battery fully charged*

At this point, we have tested all aspects of our board. The one aspect we haven't
tested is the wireless capabilities of the ESP32-C6 module. You should be able to test it by
grabbing one of the samples we have discussed in Chapters 1 and 4.

In Chapter 1, we promised to discuss code samples using the Arduino IDE. In
the next section, we will demonstrate testing the sensors on this board using the
Arduino IDE.

Testing Sensors

We are going to test the sensors in C++ using the Arduino IDE. We will test the code
samples available from the library to ensure that we can retrieve the sensor data. If you
haven't installed it already, you can download and install Arduino IDE from `https://
www.arduino.cc/en/software`.

1. The first step is to install the ESP32 Board Support Package from Espressif. This can be accomplished by launching the Arduino IDE and going to Tools ➤ Boards ➤ Boards Manager and searching for ESP32. Install the *esp32* board support package by Espressif Systems (snapshot shown in Figure 7-38).

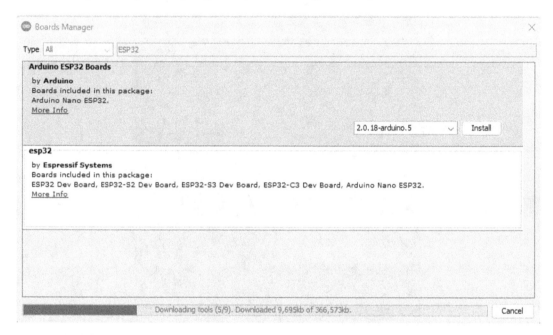

Figure 7-38. *Installing the esp32 board support package from Espressif*

2. We need to configure the connected board. It can be configured by going to Tools ➤ Boards ➤ ESP32 Arduino ➤ ESP32C6 Module as shown in Figure 7-39.

Figure 7-39. *Configure the ESP32-C6 module in Arduino IDE*

3.   We must set Tools ➤ USB CDC On Boot ➤ "Enabled" as shown in
     Figure 7-40. This would launch the serial port after resetting the
     serial port.

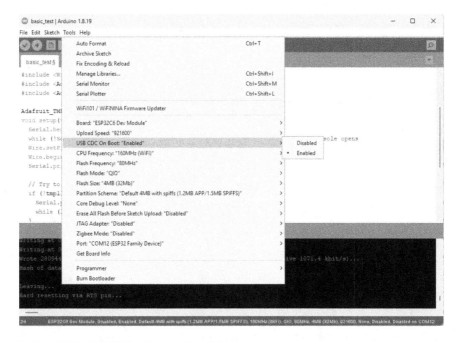

Figure 7-40. *USB CDC On Boot: Enabled*

4. Once the board support package is installed, we can install the
    libraries required to test the sensors. The libraries can be installed
    by going to Sketch ➤ Include Library ➤ Manage Libraries. We
    need to install the Adafruit TMP117 library (Figure 7-41).

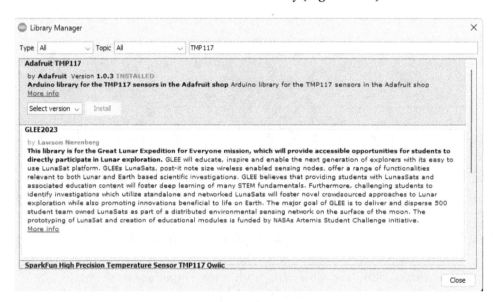

Figure 7-41. *Installing the Adafruit TMP117 library*

5. We also need to install the SparkFun MAX3010x library
    (Figure 7-42).

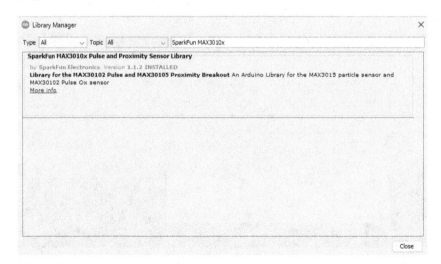

Figure 7-42. *SparkFun MAX3010x library*

Now that we have the libraries installed, we will take them for a spin and test the sensors on the board.

TMP117 Sensor Test

We can test the TMP117 sensor by loading the example installed along with the library required for this sensor. The example can be loaded from File ➤ Examples ➤ Adafruit TMP117 ➤ basic_test (Figure 7-43).

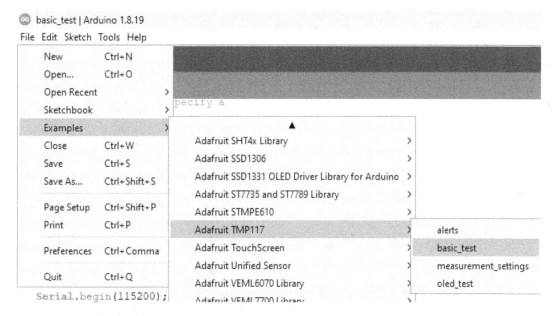

Figure 7-43. *Loading the basic test example*

We must insert two lines at the top of the setup() function to set up the I²C interface. We set the *SDA* pin to GPIO pin 3 and the *SCL* pin to GPIO pin 2 by calling the setPins() method. Then, we initialize the I²C interface by calling the begin() method:

```
Wire.setPins(3, 2);
Wire.begin();
```

When we compile and upload the sketch by using the upload button at the top, the compiled sketch is loaded on to the ESP32-C6 module as shown in Figure 7-44. If you uploaded MicroPython binary onto your board, you may have to put the module into bootloader mode using the *BOOT* button.

```
basic_test | Arduino 1.8.19
File Edit Sketch Tools Help

basic_test §

/**
 * @file basic_test.ino
 * @author Bryan Siepert for Adafruit Industries
 * @brief Shows how to specify a
 * @date 2020-11-10
 *
 * @copyright Copyright (c) 2020
 *
 */
#include <Wire.h>
#include <Adafruit_TMP117.h>
#include <Adafruit_Sensor.h>

Adafruit_TMP117  tmp117;
void setup(void) {
  Wire.setPins(3, 2);
  Wire.begin();

  Serial.begin(115200);
  while (!Serial) delay(1000);      // will pause Zero, Leonardo, etc until serial console opens
  Serial.println("Adafruit TMP117 test!");

  // Try to initialize!
  if (!tmp117.begin()) {
    Serial.println("Failed to find TMP117 chip");
    while (1) { delay(10); }
  }
  Serial.println("TMP117 Found!");

}
void loop() {

  sensors_event_t temp; // create an empty event to be filled
  tmp117.getEvent(&temp); //fill the empty event object with the current measurements
  Serial.print("Temperature  "); Serial.print(temp.temperature);Serial.println(" degrees C");
```

```
Writing at 0x0004b0e3... (90 %)
Writing at 0x00050f83... (100 %)
Wrote 280944 bytes (156550 compressed) at 0x00010000 in 2.1 seconds (effective 1071.4 kbit/s)...
Hash of data verified.

Leaving...
Hard resetting via RTS pin...
```
```
17 - 18
```

Figure 7-44. *Loading sketch onto ESP32-C6*

Once the binary is loaded, we must launch the serial monitor from the right top corner of the IDE (Figure 7-45).

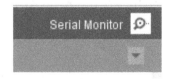

Figure 7-45. *Launching the serial monitor*

The serial monitor prints out the TMP117 sensor data (Figure 7-46).

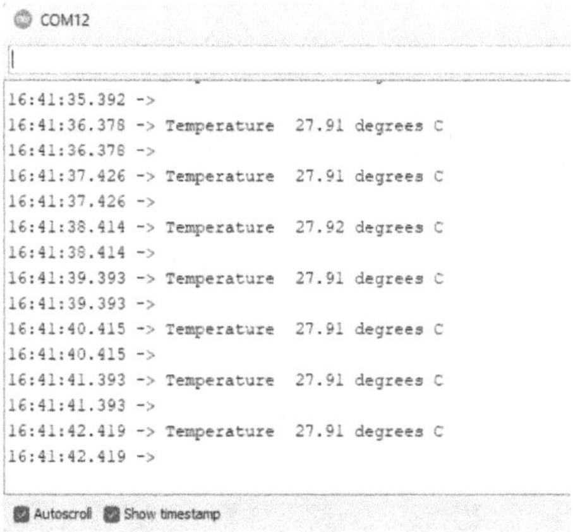

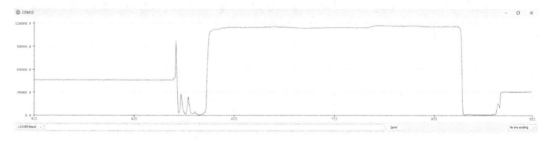

Figure 7-46. *Serial monitor data*

Now we can test the sensor by touching it with a finger and looking at the temperature variations!

MAX30102 Heart Rate Sensor

We will load the Heart Beat Plotter example from the SparkFun MAX3010x library and modify the TMP117 sensor in a similar way. Then, we upload the compiled sketch to the module and launch the Serial Plotter from Tools ➤ Serial Plotter. Once the serial plotter launches, place a finger on the heart rate sensor and observe the measurements. Figure 7-47 shows the MAX30102 sensor output on the Arduino Serial Plotter.

Figure 7-47. *Heart rate sensor raw ADC output*

We have finished testing the sensors and the board bring-up process. Since we have a working prototype, we should be able to get started with developing firmware for this device.

Power Profiling

Since this is a battery-powered device, we need to profile its current consumption. We used a current profiler (shown in Figure 7-48) to look at the current consumption under normal operating conditions while the device is in deep sleep. The device consumes around 30 mA during normal operating conditions and around 10 mA during sleep. The sleep current is higher because we aren't turning off the power to the pull-up resistors during deep sleep. Adding a switch for the pull-up resistors should reduce the sleep current to the order of microamperes. In the next iteration of this design, we can add a switch for the pull-up resistors along with other design refinements.

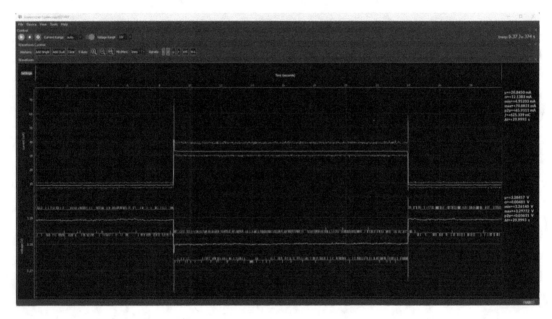

Figure 7-48. *Current profiler output*

Product Development Considerations

Now that we have a working prototype, we will consider some key factors to keep in mind as we develop it into a product.

Component Placement

When we planned a prototype for this chapter, we chose a design that could be fabricated with some effort. We decided to use a double-sided PCB design instead of a rigid-flex PCB-based design to reduce fabrication costs. A rigid-flex PCB design makes sense in the production version, where the sensors are on a second board while the ESP32 module is placed on the main board.

Redundant Components

Since this is the first iteration that would be used for firmware development, we added a USB connector, switch, etc. This might not be needed in the final version.

Enclosure Cutouts

The 3D model of the PCB can be used by mechanical engineers to modify the enclosure. For example, determine cutouts for battery connectors, external sensors, etc.

Display Interface

For this prototype, we chose to ignore adding a display to our product. If your product requires a display like most wearables do, there are ESP32 wearable development kits (shown in Figure 7-49) to get started. It must be noted that they are just development kits, and consumer-grade wearable products need to undergo a rigorous testing and certification process.

Figure 7-49. *ESP32 wearable development kits*

Project Complications

One iteration of the prototype took us nearly four weeks to finish. While planning a product's roadmap, it is safe to assume that a hardware project can take twice as long and cost twice as much as the Bill of Materials costs before it hits the shelf. So every component that is added to the product can become a bottleneck. We ignored the display in this prototype because it can be the most expensive component to integrate into a wearable. Apart from choosing a display, we also need to consider how it is going to be assembled into the enclosure, wear style, etc.

Compliance Engineering

Regulatory certification can take a long time to finish. We recommend engaging a compliance engineer to understand the certification process for your product.

Battery Selection

Since this is the product's first iteration, we didn't select a battery for the prototype, which can over-constrain the design. Once the prototype takes some shape, battery selection comes into play.

Enclosure Assembly

It is time to assemble the wearable into an enclosure (shown in Figure 7-50), take it for a spin, and try to understand what works and doesn't for this prototype. We must develop an understanding of whether this meets our customers' needs. We recommend sporting this wearable that has no display and see what people make of it.

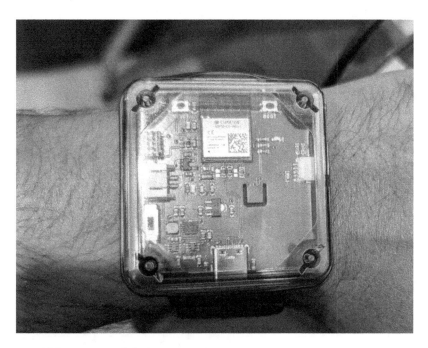

Figure 7-50. *ESP32 wearable in action!*

Conclusion

We hope you enjoyed this journey of learning product development with the ESP32 microcontroller. In the past seven chapters, we explored the powerful features of the ESP32 microcontroller and MicroPython. In this chapter, we took a wearable idea and built a prototype. We explored what it would take to capture a schematic, perform PCB layout, work with manufacturers to fabricate it, and build the first prototype.

The one lesson we have learned from developing IoT products in our career is putting a prototype in the hands of the customer, which can help understand their needs. Sometimes, it is required to give up certain requirements to keep the costs low, and the customer might recognize that certain requirements might not be necessary.

We hope you have fun building with ESP32 microcontrollers and MicroPython!

Index

A

Adafruit Anemometer Kit, 48
Adafruit ESP32-S3 Feather, 8, 9
Adafruit IO account, 64
Adafruit Metro ESP32-S3, 9–12, 31, 45, 50,
    58, 80, 82, 89, 91–93, 95, 100, 110
  I²C bus, 90, 92–95
  IDE, 17–22
  numerical order, 12
  programming language options, 15, 16
Adafruit TMP117 library, 234
AirNow API, 71, 74, 87, 88
Air quality index, 78
Air quality visual aid, 72, 108
  components, 73, 74
  description, 72, 73
  retrieving data, 74–88
  sensors, 89–109
Antenna assembly, 145, 146
Application Programming
    Interface (API)
  obtaining, 75
  script, 87
  test query, 75–79
Arduino, 5, 9, 11, 15
  shields, 14
  support package, 15
Arduino IDE, 16, 25, 191, 192
  ESP32 Board Support Package, 22–24
  LED Blinky, 31–34
Autodesk Eagle, 219

B

Battery connector, 214
Bill of materials, 224, 225
bluetooth_client_task(), 138
Bluetooth low energy
    (BLE), 7, 124
  devices, 119
  on ESP32, 119, 120
  protocols, 119
Bluetooth products
  bluetooth/Wi-Fi
    gateway, 136–140
  components, 120
  sensor integration, 120–136
Bluetooth sensor node
  bluetooth/Wi-Fi
    gateway, 136–140
  code sample
    discussion, 126–136
  prerequisite libraries, 124–126
Board bring-up, 227–230
  binary and resetting, 228
  ESP32-C6 module, 228
  LED blinking test, 230
  MAX30102 heart rate sensor, 237
  testing sensors, 231–235
  TMP117 sensor, 235–237
Board selection, 11, 12
Board shape import, 219, 220
Bootstrapping pins, 208
Buck-boost regulator, 216

C

Chart blocks, 67
CircuitPython, 16
Cloud Iintegration, 6
Compliance engineering, 164, 240
Component placement and layout
    bill of materials, 224, 225
    board layout, 221, 222
    board stack-up, 220
    verification, 222–224

D

Dashboard
    highlighting units, 69
    settings, 64
        chart blocks, 67
        creation, 65
        edit layout, 68
        sensors stream, 66
        weather station, 69
Data analysis, 170
Dataset building, 174–195
Debugging, 209
Deployment, 170
Development kits, 5

E

Edge impulse, 172
    applications, 194
    dataset building, 174–195
    hardware requirements, 172, 173
Enclosure assembly, 240, 241
End-of-life (EOL), 116
ESP32 Board Support Package, 22–24
ESP32-CAM module, 173
ESP32 LoRa Gateway, 156–162

ESP32 LoRa Sensor Node, 152–156
ESP32 microcontroller, 116, 135, 136, 167,
        170, 172, 203, 206, 241
    advantages, 3–6
    applications, 1
    bluetooth capabilities, 39–43
    bluetooth/Wi-Fi
        gateway, 136–140
    development board, 7, 8
    documents downloading, 25, 26
    interactive tool, 2
    LED Blinky, 31–40
    module-based development
        board, 8–12
    module variant selection, 7
    power profiling, 140–142
    variants, 2, 3
    weather station, 1
    Wi-Fi examples, 35–39
ESP32Pedometer class, 128
ESP32-S3-DEVKITC-1-N8, 10
ESP32-S3 Feather, 8, 9
ESP32-S3-WROOM-1
        module, 9, 10, 13
ESP-IDF framework, 15
Espressif systems, 2, 196

F

Fitness machine service, 134

G, H

Gerber file generation, 224
get_modem() function, 157
get_value method, 61
GPIO pin 13, 25, 26, 28, 32
Graphics Processing Unit (GPU), 167

I

I²C Communication
Interface, 90, 91, 205, 209
bus scan, 92
devices, 91
SCD41 and SEN55, 96
sensirion sensors, 98–100
Image classification
hardware, 172, 173
input() function, 84
Integrated Development
Environment (IDE)
Arduino IDE, 22–24
MicroPython installation, 17–22
Thonny IDE, 17
Internet of Things (IoT), 1
IP address, 83
irq_callback, 41

J, K

JSON format, 60

L

Lark Weather Station, 47
LED Blinky
Arduino IDE, 31–34
using MicroPython, 25–31
Long-range radios (LoRa), 143
antenna assembly, 145, 146
breakout board, 148–152
components, 143, 144
library installation, 144, 145
RFM95W breakout, 146–148
sensor data aggregation, 152–162
loop() function, 32
LoRaWAN networks

cellular modules, 163, 164
heatmap, 162
low-power devices, 162
MIT license, 163
LSM6DS3 sensor, 120

M

MAX30102 sensor, 205, 212, 213, 237
MicroPython, 15, 16
air quality data
retrieval, 82–88
code sample, 55
driver, 50, 95
I²C driver, 96
installation, 17–22
interpreter, 19, 30, 229
LED Blinky, 25–31
package, 144
repository, 40, 126
secrets.py, 79–82
Micro speech, 196
MIT license, 50

N

Network module, 83

O

Ozone (O_3), 77

P

Parameters, 59, 83
pinMode function, 32
post_data() function, 157
post_data() method, 138

Power circuitry
    battery charging circuit, 215
    battery connector and switch, 214
    buck-boost converter, 216
    USB-C connector, 214, 215
    1.8V low-dropout (LDO) regulator, 216, 217
Power profiling, 140–142, 238, 239
Pre-certified modules, 5
Prerequisite installation, 196–200
Product building
    assembly confirmation, 227
    board shape import, 219, 220
    bootstrapping pins, 208
    component placement and layout, 219–226
    components, 204
    debugging circuitry, 209
    development, 239
    electrical rule check, 217, 218
    enclosure selection, 218
    ESP32-module selection, 206
    filtering & decoupling capacitors, 207
    interrupt pins, 210
    MAX30102, 205
    PCB layout, 218–227
    power circuitry, 214–217
    quote generation, 226, 227
    Qwiic connect system, 213
    real-time clock, 211
    requirements, 204
    reset circuit, 207, 208
    schematic capture process, 205, 206
    sensors selection, 205
    TMP117 sensor, 205, 211, 212
    USB interface, 209
Product development

battery selection, 240
compliance engineering, 240
component placement, 239
display interface, 239
enclosure cutouts, 239
project complications, 240
redundant components, 239
Prototyping, 11

Q

Qwiic connect system, 91, 92, 213

R

Receiver (RX) pin, 48
Refinement, 171
Remote monitoring application, 168
Retrieving data
    API, 79–83
    data use guidelines, 88
    MicroPython, 79–88
RFM95W breakout, 146–148

S

scan() method, 35, 94
SCD41 sensor, 74, 89, 94, 95, 105–109
Schematic capture process, 205, 206
secrets.py, 79–82
SEN55 sensor, 74, 89, 94, 95, 100–105
Sensor data aggregation
    ESP32 LoRa Gateway, 156–162
    ESP32 LoRa Sensor Node, 152–156
Sensor integration
    setting up UART interface, 48–50
    weather station kit, 50–52
Sensors

air quality
    I²C (Inter-Integrated Circuit, 90, 91
    prerequisite libraries, 96, 97
    Qwiic connect system, 91, 92
    SCD41 and SEN55, 95
    SCD41 driver, 105–109
    selection, 89, 90
    SEN55 driver, 100–105
    sensirion-i²c-driver, 98–100
feeds, 53
integration
    bluetooth sensor node, 124–136
    driver test, 122–124
    ESP32-S3, 120
selection, 47, 48, 205
SparkFun Indoor Air Quality Combo
    Sensor, 89
stream, 66
testing, 231–235
Serial data clock (SCL), 90
Serial data line (SDA), 90
16 MB of Octal SPI Flash, 17
16 MB of Quad SPI Flash, 17
SMA antenna connector, 145
SparkFun Indoor Air Quality Combo
    Sensor, 89, 92–95
SparkFun Weather Meter Kit, 48
Stemma/Qwiic connector, 14

T

TensorFlow MicroPython, 172
Test query, 75–79
Thonny IDE, 17, 19, 56, 79, 80, 104,
    107, 144
Tiny Machine Learning (TinyML), 167
    advantages, 169
    code sample, 196

data point, 168
datasets, 171
development, 170, 171
image classification, 172–194
IoT application, 167
prerequisite installation, 196–200
product development, 200, 201
remote monitoring
    application, 168
schematic, 195, 196
sensor data point, 168
toolsets, 171–173
TMP117 sensor, 205, 211,
    212, 235–237
Transmitter (TX), 48

U

UART interface, 48, 49
    settings, 49, 50
Unique Identifiers (UUID), 127
USB interface, 209

V

Visual aid
    code, 110–114
    device provisioning, 116
    display driver, 108–110
    enclosure design, 115
    LVGL, 114, 115
    manufacturing, 116
    product pricing, 115
    revenue model, 115
    servicing, 117
    sourcing components, 116
    time to market, 116
1.8V low-dropout (LDO), 216, 217

W, X, Y, Z

Wearable prototype, 203
Weather station
    components, 47
    dashboard setup, 64–69
    data publishing, 53–70
    description, 45–47
    installation, 69
    sensor integration, 48–52
    sensor selection, 47, 48

Weather station kit, 50–52
Webhooks, 54, 55, 58–64
Wide user base, 6
Wi-Fi, 56, 58, 60
    connection, 37–39
    gateway, 136–140
    network, 85, 86, 124
    range, 152
    scanner, 35–37

GPSR Compliance
The European Union's (EU) General Product Safety Regulation (GPSR) is a set
of rules that requires consumer products to be safe and our obligations to
ensure this.

If you have any concerns about our products, you can contact us on

ProductSafety@springernature.com

In case Publisher is established outside the EU, the EU authorized
representative is:

Springer Nature Customer Service Center GmbH
Europaplatz 3
69115 Heidelberg, Germany